AIRLINER TECH SERIES

VOLUME 3

GW00568023

AIRBUS INDUSTRIE
AIRBUS A340

BY SCOTT E. GERMAIN

specialtypress
PUBLISHERS AND WHOLESALERS

Published by
Specialty Press Publishers and Wholesalers
11605 Kost Dam Road
North Branch, MN 55056
United States of America
(651) 583-3239

Distributed in the UK and Europe by
Airlife Publishing Ltd.
101 Longden Road
Shrewsbury
SY3 9EB
England

ISBN 1-58007-002-7

Designed by Dennis R. Jenkins

Printed in the United States of America

Front Cover: The A340's wings are thick and long; optimized for efficient, long-range flight. The thickness allows for a strong structure with plenty of volume for fuel. (Airbus)

Back Cover (Left Top): Singapore Airline's attractive 50th Anniversary paint scheme is shown during pushback from the gate. During the pushback, the APU supplies enough bleed air to start two engines at the same time. This makes for quick and efficient running of the After Start and Taxi checks. (P. Johnston)

Back Cover (Right Top): A variety of entertainment options are available, including personal LCD screens . (Airbus)

Back Cover (Lower): Airbus spent numerous hours of human factors research and developed a new philosophy in cockpit design and integration for the earlier A320. In the interest of commonality, the A340's cockpit is almost an exact copy. (Airbus)

TABLE OF CONTENTS

THE AIRBUS A340

AIRBUS INDUSTRIE
AIRBUS A340

PREFACE

ACKNOWLEDGEMENTS

I am fortunate in that I get to do something I love for a living.

I used to be the kid at the airport fence, gazing at the general aviation aircraft that I would eventually learn to fly. My dreams were aimed at flying "warbirds" – restored World War II aircraft – and racing unlimiteds at Reno. I didn't give much thought to the PSA Boeing 727s lifting off Burbank's runway 15, or the bright yellow paint schemes of the Hughes Airwest DC-9s. In fact, piloting these jets seemed like a far off dream, something to be thought about at a later date.

As I grew older and added ratings and licenses to my airman ticket, plans were made that would lead me to the cockpit of a commercial airliner. Who would I fly for? What equipment would I fly? Thoughts drifted to the classic Boeing 737, the workhorse of today's airlines. Perhaps I would fly McDonnell Douglas' MD-80, an elegant and popular aircraft as well. Later in my career, I might have an opportunity to fly a wide-body aircraft such as the 747 or L-1011. The possibilities, as dealt by fate, could be endless. It was an exciting dream.

I can't remember when I first heard of Airbus Industrie, but the aura surrounding the European consortium was a negative one. "If it's not Boeing, I'm not going!" was a battle cry in the skies above the United States. They were a threat to our superiority in aerospace, and many bought into it. I remained neutral.

It is ironic the first jet I would come to operate for a major airline would be the Airbus A320. I had no preconceived notions about learning the systems and flying the aircraft, so my mind was a sponge, willing to soak up everything. I had no bad habits to unlearn, and no rival design philosophies to cling to. My impression of Airbus' way of doing things is extremely favorable.

Yes; Boeing and Airbus design aircraft in different manners. Politics play a role. I am not party to any of these processes, and this book contains no reference to boardroom/war room tactics or smear campaigns. I'm a pilot pure and simple, so you will get a pilot's eye view of an excellent aircraft; the Airbus A340.

Even though I fly the A340's little brother, writing about the larger aircraft made me realize the genius behind Airbus' philosophy. The A318, 319, 320, 321, 330, and 340 are simply the most technologically advanced civilian aircraft in the skies today, and provide true commonality to their operators. I hope you will find a level of awe and excitement beneath the skin of the A340, as I did.

I'd like to thank Mark Luginbill and Captain Larry Rockliff of Airbus. Both of these gentlemen provided me with invaluable materials on the A340; an aircraft new enough that little can be found in current aviation databases. Special thanks go to Captain Rockliff, who suffered through an hour of my flying an A340 full-motion simulator on two hours of sleep. There's bravery for you. Thanks also to A330/340 Program Manager Alan Pardoe at Airbus in Toulouse, France, for sharing a wealth of information on the A340 program. David Velupillai, Airbus' Regional Manager for Press Relations, also provided invaluable technical and material assistance. Rudy Canto, also with Airbus, provided technical details relating to flying the A340. Thank you all very much.

Thanks also go to Nick Veronico, a personal friend and noted aviation author, who provided information and contacts that added greatly to this text. Thanks to John Hicks, Superintendent of Operations at LAX for getting me airside to photograph the A340, as well as Ron Wilson and Chappie Solomon at SFO for doing the same. Thanks to Cathay Pacific pilot Aaron Rogers for sharing A340 system information, and to James Steiner for A340 pamphlets and safety cards. A number of aviation enthusiasts have shared their A340 photos with me, and they are noted in the photo credits throughout the book. Thank you all very much.

Scott E. Germain
August, 1999

AIRBUS INDUSTRIE

A340

A340

AIRBUS A340

DEVELOPMENT

When an aviation enthusiast is asked to picture a battle for the skies, one might conjure up images of fighters engaged in an epic aerial dogfight. Set in any era, the proper aircraft types can be brought to mind to create vivid imagery to answer the question. By shifting to the 1990s and further refining it with the word "civilian," one might picture the mighty Boeing battling – and finally acquiring – McDonnell Douglas. Other early and historic commercial jet manufacturers, including Lockheed, De Havilland, and British Aerospace would either exit the market or become partners in larger companies.

Amid the battles for production orders throughout the '70s and '80s, a new manufacturer materialized. Airbus Industrie formed in the early 1970s with French, German, Spanish, and British partners. The goal of the European consortium widely focused on saving the historic and valuable aerospace industry within Europe. More importantly, the group aimed to capture a fifty-percent share of the lucrative jet transport market. This would eventually occur as the result of strong business sense and the ability to build world-class aircraft.

Through the early years, Airbus achieved short-term goals with the A300 and the later A310, both twinjet wide-bodies. These aircraft were the first of their type, creating a new way of thinking and defining a new aircraft market. Boeing would follow suit with its 757 and 767 designs.

Today, aviation enthusiasts have no doubt become familiar with Airbus Industrie, one of the two major commercial jet producers to survive. A wide range of commercial transport aircraft have propelled Airbus into a position to take on the Boeing giant on even terms. The glamourous dogfights of yesteryear gave way to a battle between Boeing and Airbus. The maneuvering would occur in airline boardrooms and in headquarters across the globe. The weapons of choice had become aircraft performance figures, cost analysis, financing, and contracts.

Airbus' first product was the A300, a high capacity twin for regional routes. The design philosophy of the aircraft has filtered down through the A320 program and is in use on the A330/340. (Airbus)

The A310 further expanded the Airbus product line and built a solid customer base around the world. A310s are still in widespread passenger and cargo use around the world, with American FedEx being the largest operator. (Airbus)

Shaping the A340

Jetliner production in the United States is a proud heritage shared by Boeing, Lockheed, and McDonnell Douglas. Through the post-World War II years, they were the world's jetliner manufacturers. Relatively unchallenged, thousands of 7-7s, DCs, and TriStars racked up millions of air miles, and earned the trust of pilots, mechanics, and not least of all, the traveling public. Except for Concorde, the absence of a strong European manufacturer was apparent.

The genesis of Airbus Industrie is well documented elsewhere. The company's success in the early years was the result of identifying and filling market niches left by the "Americans," as the French like to put it. The A300 and A310 were positioned as the first twin-engine wide-body aircraft, but Airbus wanted to build a large wide-body jet to expand the product line.

The design that would become the A340 was aimed at entering the long-range market. The new aircraft would be the size of the DC-10 or L-1011 with the range of a 747. Although these first-generation wide-bodies are excellent, reliable, and proven aircraft in every right, technology had greatly advanced in the 1980s and 1990s. New designs could capitalize on more efficient engines and aerodynamics, as well as new design methods, composite materials, and avionics.

B9 and B11 Concepts

In the early 1970s, Airbus considered several different options to compliment the wide-body product line. The brainstorm of ideas that accompanied the A300 and A310 aircraft included designs dubbed B9 and B11, paper aircraft based firmly in 1970s technology. The B9 was a stretched A300 twinjet with the most powerful engines available at the time. The B11 was a similar aircraft with four engines aimed at long routes that would not support a 747. It would also replace aging and less efficient 707, DC-8, L-1011, and early 747 aircraft. The B11 was a more drastic change from the base A300 model, and featured a new wing design with increased span, a shorter fuselage, and four early CFM56 engines in the 22,000 lb. thrust class.

Viewed as a product line, the A300, A310, B9, and B11 models would constitute a comprehensive wide-body family that would fuel Airbus production well through the year 2000. In planning Airbus' strategy, early Airbus Chief Executive Roger Beteille stated, "I do not have the slightest doubt about it. We simply have to build the new wide-bodies." As early as 1975, Beteille and Chairman Henri Ziegler bore the idea that these wide-bodies would be designed with a high level of commonality with other Airbus aircraft; future designs or otherwise. These early signs of an integrated Airbus family would be fully realized when the A340 entered service.

But the time was simply not right. The market and economic climate favored the design and production of a smaller aircraft, which became the Single-Aisle (SA) A320. This clean-sheet design utilized a new generation of electronic avionics and a digital flight management system, making it the most advanced airliner in the skies. The A320 series also brought Airbus wider recognition by more airlines more quickly than a long-range aircraft would have. Simply put, the A320 was the right aircraft – both for Airbus and the market – at the right time. Although the lucrative big jets had been pushed aside for the 150 seat A320, their turn was about to come.

A320 production began in 1984, with brisk sales in Europe, North America, and across the globe. Airbus had made inroads to the American market with the A300, and furthered a foothold with A320 orders

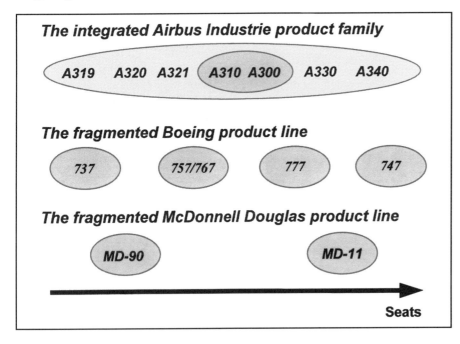

The integrated Airbus Industrie product family

A319 A320 A321 A310 A300 A330 A340

The fragmented Boeing product line

737   757/767   777   747

The fragmented McDonnell Douglas product line

MD-90   MD-11

Seats

Comparison between Airbus, Boeing, and McDonnell Douglas product lines. (Airbus)

"The Right Aircraft and the Right Time." Airbus gambled wisely when the go-ahead was given to the A320 program. The aircraft, and its larger and smaller derivatives cover markets from 100 seats to 180 seats. (Airbus)

from America West, United, and Northwest Airlines. Even though the American economy at the time was sluggish, conditions worldwide began to ripen for a new long-range wide-body.

Airbus kept updating the B9 and B11 concepts as advances in aerodynamics, avionics, and engine technologies became available. As of 1977, the B11 design became better defined. The aircraft featured a long-span wing for extended range, and the same 222 inch fuselage diameter as the A310. Using the same cross section would cut development costs and allow Airbus to manufacture the sections on tooling already in hand.

Further research determined that both the B9 and B11 models could even share the same wing. The twin-

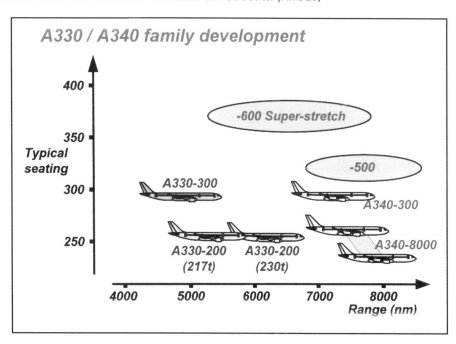

A330/340 market coverage in terms of seat and range. The A340-8000 has been combined with the A340-500 specification. (Airbus)

Airbus had proven itself with the A300/A310 aircraft, and saw a golden opportunity to capture a large portion of the 150 seat market. The decision to produce the A320 and its derivatives proved to be the correct one. Over 1,000 of the single-aisle twin jets, like this A321, have been produced. (Airbus)

jet B9 and the quad-jet B11 were shaping up to be very similar aircraft, although each was aimed at a different market. By choosing to develop these two aircraft in parallel, Airbus would realize drastic cuts in development costs and could cover different markets with aircraft from the same production line. Development costs for the joint program were forecast at approximately $3.5 billion dollars.

In 1980, the B9 and B11 designations were changed to TA9 and TA11 respectively to signify the fact that they were Twin-Aisle wide-bodies. Up to this point, Airbus products

had strictly been twin-engined, but studies were made to investigate the use of three 37,000 lb. thrust Rolls Royce 535 or Pratt and Whitney PW2000 engines for the long-range aircraft. At one point, the 230-410 seat-jets were enlarged and given four engines in the same 35,000 lb. thrust class, a sign of how the program would ultimately shape up.

The changes in the B9 and B11 aircraft indicated the level of flux in the marketplace. Balancing market demands is difficult even on the best of days. World economies, fuel prices, currency exchange rates, and above all, evolving travel demands

were mixing to help shape the new aircraft. One unexpected development Airbus met with was the growth of the A300 and A310 aircraft. Design improvements allowed these jets to carry heavier loads farther than anybody had envisioned. At the same time, most DC-8 operators were choosing to re-engine with the more efficient CFM56. Although much older designs without the benefit of a large fuselage cross-section, these aircraft were biting into the perceived TA11 market.

The TA11 and TA12 were showcased as 220-270 seat transports of mixed class cabin layouts and underfloor cargo space for 17 LD3 containers. The TA11 would be powered by four engines in the 30,000 - 34,000 lb. thrust category, and was intended for oceanic sectors up to 6,830 nautical miles. Although these performance numbers and capabilities were impressive, the prevailing economy had produced a glut of long-range trijets on the used market. Airbus executives forecasted the market for the TA11 design would arrive sometime in the early 1990s.

Commonality

Airbus had taken a hard look at TA designs, and realized their commonality idea could be employed perfectly within this program. Using

---

Airbus published revised specifications at the 1982 Farnborough Air Show for the TA9, TA11, and a twin-engine TA11 derivative called the TA12. These were:

TA9:
326 to 410 passengers
two 60,000 lb./thrust engines
A300-600-based fuselage
New wing
30 underfloor LD3s
1,500 - 3,300 nm range

TA11-100:
230 passengers
four 34,000 lb./thrust engines
A310-based fuselage
New wing
17 underfloor LD3s
6,830 nm range

TA11-200:
270 passengers
four 34,000 lb./thrust engines
A310-based fuselage
New wing
24 underfloor LD3s
6,830 nm range

TA12:
220 passengers
two 62,000 lb./thrust engines
A310-based fuselage
New wing

basically the same A310 fuselage cross section with added barrel sections, the TA9 and TA11 aircraft would employ a common wing, systems, and as many off-the-shelf items as possible, yet serve widely different markets. The same production line would manufacture the aircraft, and any future derivatives that would inevitably come. Commonality would also mean very similar flight and handling characteristics with the A320.

Various events were further honing the shape and capability of the TA11. Falling fuel prices, the preference of a three-class cabin layout, and the rising expectations of comfort and amenities from passengers were redefining the shape of the new aircraft and how it would be used. Airbus fully understood the value of input from prospective airline buyers and lent a serious ear.

Obviously, if potential customers have a hand in the design of the product, they are more likely to buy it. Alan Pardoe, current Product Manager/Marketing of the A330/340 program explains, "Hopefully, we are 100% market driven when it comes to aircraft design. The customer airlines quite clearly define what the range, capacity, runway performance, and payload ought to be. Regarding the A340, they spelled a lot of things out, and we responded by incorporating these requirements into the design of the airplane." Airbus was basing costs and vendor agreements on a production run of 800 aircraft over the years, but hoped for 1,000.

Caught with the landing gear retracting, Air Canada's A340-300 C-GDVV gets airborne. The main landing gear bogies compress six inches as they retract inward, while both fuselage landing gear retract forward.
(George Polfliet)

Lufthansa A340-200 D-AIBA wears partial paint schemes of Star Alliance partners SAS, Thai, Varig, Air Canada, and United. Today's complex code-share agreements blur the lines of different carriers when passengers buy tickets, but certainly lead to interesting liveries. (George Polfliet)

🌀 A340-300 underfloor hold capability

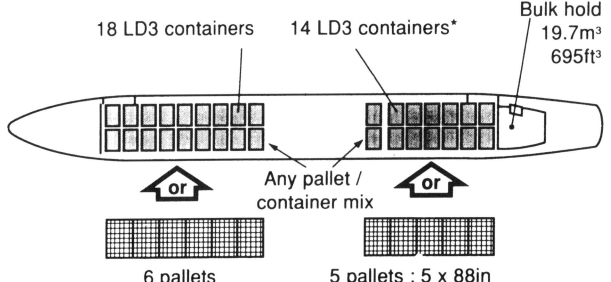

18 LD3 containers

14 LD3 containers*

Bulk hold
19.7m³
695ft³

Any pallet /
container mix

or

or

6 pallets
(88 or 96in)

5 pallets : 5 x 88in
or 5 pallets : 3 x 96in + 2 x 88in
or 4 pallets : 4 x 96in + 2 LD3

Standard aircraft has large forward and aft cargo doors

*Option : additional LD3 in bulk hold; remaining bulk volume 486ft³ (13.8m³)

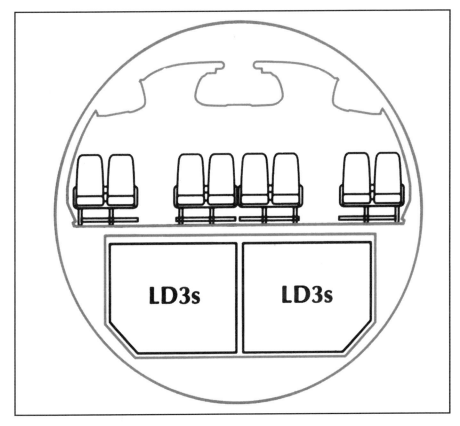

LD3s   LD3s

The amount of under-floor cargo space in the A340 series is popular with the airlines, as large amounts of revenue are generated below the cabin floor. (Airbus)

Space within the A340's 222-inch diameter fuselage is utilized well, with dead space kept to a minimum. The eight-abreast seating greatly increases the number of passengers with an aisle or window seat, and prevents the "double excuse me" center seat on nine-abreast configurations. (Airbus)

Preliminary Go-Ahead

Boeing continued to move towards larger aircraft with the launch of the 747-300. This development widened the market niche between the wide-body tri-jets and the new 747. Airbus immediately realized the time had come for its new transports. The TA9 and TA11 were positioned perfectly for this opportunity.

Historically, the Paris Air Show has been a stage for the introduction of new aircraft to the world market, and the announcement of new orders. Unfortunately, Airbus was not in a position to formally announce the program yet, but the company used the 1985 event to disburse information to potential customers. Literature showed the four TA concepts had been streamlined back to a more capable twin-engine TA9 aircraft, and the four-engine TA11.

What the airlines saw were two new aircraft that shared the same airframe with minimum changes. The changes in the number of engines and related systems would define how the aircraft would be used. According to Airbus, long routes are better served by four engines, while short to medium routes are better served by a twin-engine design. With the TA9 and TA11 concepts, Airbus had covered all the bases. Only slight differences in the wing would be necessary between the TA9 and TA11, mostly involving support for the additional engines and fuel tankage. The TA11 would require more fuel for long-range operations, so its wing was tailored to carry fuel in the center section. A

An early goal of Airbus engineers was to provide passengers with business-class seats that were wide and comfortable. Foot rests and recline functions for sleeping were also included. A variety of inflight entertainment options are available, from personal LCD screens and headphones to the ceiling mounted projector. (Airbus)

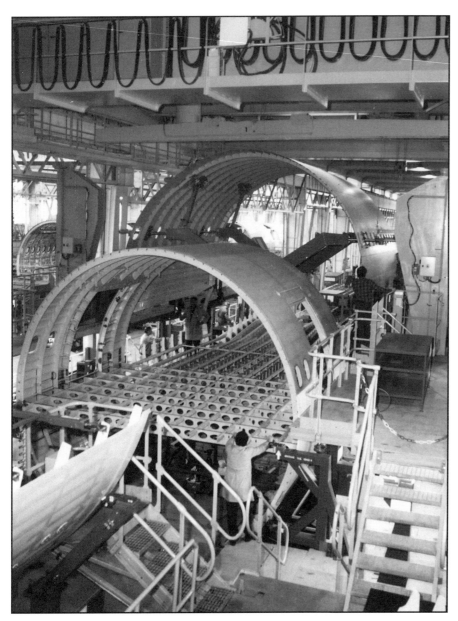

The common fuselage for the TA9 and TA11 aircraft would be manufactured at Aerospatiale's St. Nazaire facility. When the program was launched, the TA11 was transformed into the A340. These center fuselage sections are the longest of any Airbus aircraft. (Airbus)

center mounted landing gear was also incorporated under the fuselage to help support the higher design weight of the aircraft.

Airbus engineers fought hard to achieve the same seat-mile costs of the latest 747 with an aircraft that contained 33% fewer seats. The TA 11 would accommodate 250 passengers in three cabin classes over stage lengths of 6,500 nautical miles. Overwater ETOPS restrictions would be avoided due to the four-engine configuration, and takeoff performance in hot-and-high conditions would also prove to be excellent.

On January 27, 1986, the Airbus Industrie Supervisory Board met in Munich, Germany to finalize and approve the future strategy for completing the product line. Board Chairman Dr. Franz-Joseph Strauss announced, "Airbus Industrie is now in a position to finalize the detailed

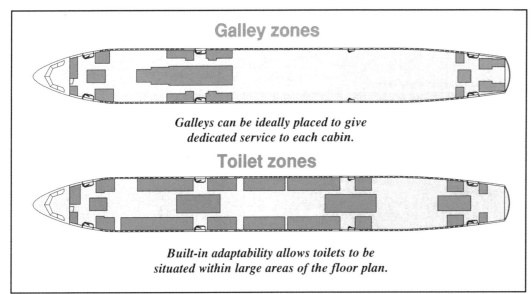

Galley zones

Galleys can be ideally placed to give dedicated service to each cabin.

Toilet zones

Built-in adaptability allows toilets to be situated within large areas of the floor plan.

Engineers designed the cabin of the A340 to be highly flexible in terms of galley and toilet placement. Airlines can order any cabin combination that suits their needs, and have the flexibility to change it later. (Airbus)

technical definition of the TA9, which is now officially designated as the A330, and the TA11, now called the A340, with potential customer airlines, and to discuss with them the terms and conditions for launch commitments."

Although not a formal launch announcement, the long-standing dream of producing a wide-body, long-range jet was drawing close. Airbus strategy had proven correct; the family of aircraft would now cover routes between 300 and 7,000 nm and capacities between 107 and over 400 seats. The A330/340 program, viewed as virtually one aircraft by the company, would mark the last significant investment of the millennium for a new Airbus transport.

During 1986, Airbus continued to develop the A340 at an increased rate. At company headquarters in Toulouse, France, a fifty-person Integrated Task Force comprised the technical core of the development team, with similar but unduplicated work performed at the partner companies.

The A340 featured a digital Fly By Wire (FBW) system based on the A320 system. In keeping with aircraft commonality, the A340 also shared much of the cockpit design and autoflight capability of the A320, as well as similar flight characteristics. The passenger cabin had the ability to quickly change seating, galley and lavatory layouts, and to integrate personal entertainment systems into the seats.

Advanced Wing

Early in the program, new ideas and technologies were incorporated into the A340 wing as they became available. The wing would be the largest ever designed and built in the United Kingdom, or Western Europe for that matter. The development

Usually the area that is compromised in aircraft design: the galley. In the A340, a wide aisle allows flight attendants to easily move around during meal preparation. Large cart stowage areas are provided, with ovens and coffee makers installed on the upper shelf. (Airbus)

effort was led by British Aerospace Chief Designer Sid Wadling, along with Jeff Jupp and Andy Carlile. Based at the Bristol facility, these men and their engineering team would design the entire wing and main landing gear attach points for the A330/340. Wing production would occur at the BAe Broughton plant. Although the same wing equips both the A330 and A340, there is only a 2% difference in structural content between the two aircraft.

The wing was already optimized for low-drag, long-range operations, but studies continued to make the wing more efficient. British Aerospace had designed and built every wing ever installed on an Airbus, and obviously possessed a wealth of data to work with. During wind tunnel tests of the A310 wing, aerodynamicists had found that a sculpted,

downward camber built into the trailing edge allowed the aircraft to carry an additional 11,000 lbs. of payload or fuel. Overall lift increased by eight percent despite simplifying the flaps and removing their trailing edge tabs.

Airbus called this an "Aft-Loaded Airfoil," a concept similar to a supercritical wing. Engineers also designed the A340 wing to generate several smaller shock waves, instead of one large one. The wing was also quite deep, allowing the actual structure to be light, more efficient, and capable of holding large quantities of fuel. Since the A340 wing was going to spend most of its time in cruising, a high aspect-ratio planform was chosen. This long, relatively short-chord wing is characterized by low induced drag figures, which suit the A340's mission perfectly.

Although the chord of the A340 wing was relatively short, the chosen cross section of the airfoil was deeper than most aerodynamicists would like. Even though a thicker wing tends to produce more drag, the wing team had overcome this drawback and actually achieved a divergent Mach number (M_{DIV}) of a thinner airfoil. The end result was a thick, relatively light wing able to carry sufficient fuel at a respectable cruise speed. Additionally, the beefy internal structure allowed the use of thinner aluminum sheet to

cover the wing, helpful in keeping weight to a minimum.

In comparison, the remarkable thickness to chord ratio of 12.8% bettered rival McDonnell Douglas' 8-9% on the MD-11, a reworked DC-10 tri-jet in direct competition with the A340. Since the MD-11 wing was so thin, its structure could not support much growth in span or lifting ability. Airbus had planned for this eventuality.

BAe engineers wanted to utilize the "adaptive wing" concept, at least to the degree mature technology

could support. A truly adaptive wing would change its camber like a bird to meet the needs of different flight regimes. However, limitations in structures and flexible skins, as well as the current methods of wing design and manufacturing, prevented the A340 from using true adaptive wing concepts.

Within technology's limitations, the BAe design team devised a creative system to pivot the flaps up, back and down on a programmed schedule. In essence, the flaps and slats were used to change the wing's

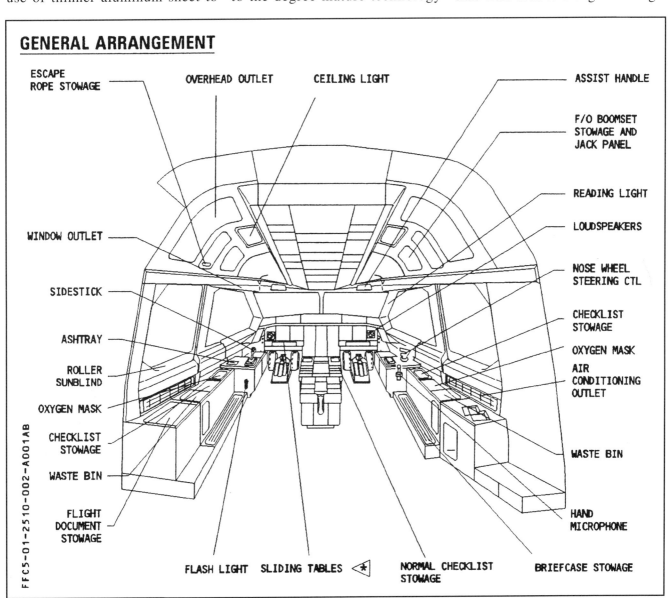

General arrangement of the A340 flight deck. (Airbus)

camber any time from liftoff through touchdown, even with large changes in aircraft weight. The end result of this flap system was a lift value close to optimum over the entire flight regime, with predictions of a two percent rise in overall aerodynamic efficiency. The pioneering system, although it deserves merit, was not used in the final wing design. Subsequent wind tunnel testing revealed that the peak aerodynamic efficiency of the wing was achieved without using this innovative feature.

Attention also focused on drag reduction by achieving laminar flow across the wings, engine pylons, and structural intersections. This undisturbed flow requires perfectly smooth wings, aerodynamic surfaces, and fairings. Problems arise in the manufacturing process when surface irregularities lead to drag producing ridges and dimples in the surface of the aircraft. Airbus overcame these problems with automated component production, assembly line robots, and strict quality control measures.

This precise design and manufacturing process resulted in a one percent improvement in the onset of high-speed Mach buffet. The early A340 wing, with only modest sweep and low structural weight, performed well at a cruise speed of Mach 0.82. The extra research allowed cruise speed to increase from 0.81 to 0.82 Mach, a fact that would net airlines significant fuel savings over the life of the aircraft. Limiting airspeed is 330 KTS and 0.86 Mach.

Future A340s may very well be equipped with lower deck sleeping quarters for premium-class passengers. Airbus is a leader in lower deck utilization ideas, with lower deck sleeping, office, and business quarters available on the A340-500 and -600. (Airbus)

During the test program, Airbus flew the A340 at widely varying weights. One of the prototypes is seen here during a "heavy" test flight, as shown by the upward flexed wings. (Airbus)

The A340 wing is a clean, efficient design allowing excellent cruise performance. The small hole on the undersurface is a fuel over-pressure port, while the vent allows air to enter the surge tank. (Scott E. Germain)

Further aerodynamic clean up concentrated on reducing the turbulent boundary layer of air that swirls about much of the surface of the aircraft. Trials are underway to assess the long term benefit of applying "riblet" film to areas of the wings, fuselage, and fin. Wind tunnel data also showed slits cut along the span of the wing allowed the boundary layer air to flow from the high pressure region downstream of the shock wave into the region ahead of it. This weakened the shock wave, reduced flow separation, and cut drag. Lift coefficient and buffet boundary figures are also improved by a perceptible margin. Some of these ideas were found implausible for a production aircraft, but the advances in automated/robotic manufacturing have allowed the A340 program to achieve very high levels of aerodynamic standards.

Close attention was paid to the turbulent boundary layer flow on the A340 wing. Even the canoe fairings that cover the trailing-edge flap tracks have been optimized so that they actually produce very little drag. (Scott E. Germain)

"Riblet" film, developed by the 3M Corporation, is currently being tested on this Cathay A340-300. The film is designed to cut down turbulent boundary layer flow. The film covers most of the wing top, the tail, and the upper fuselage. (Airbus)

ENGINE CHOICE

The closest thing to a major crisis in the A340 program came after the engine choice was finalized. Airbus had always followed a golden rule of using proven, certificated engines on aircraft. Failure to adhere to this rule cost Airbus a lot of time and money, not to mention some of its hard-earned reputation.

Several engines had been considered for the A340 program while still in the project stage. Finalists came down to several engines in the 30,000 lb. thrust class, with CFM and IAE (International Aero Engines) leading the pack. IAE, a consortium comprised of Pratt & Whitney, Rolls Royce, MTU, Fiat, and Japanese Aero Engines, had an attractive option in their V2500. The high-bypass turbofan was proving itself on the A320 with good results, but against the competing CFM56, the V2500 did not have the required thrust for the lucrative A340 program. Even though the V2500 was more fuel efficient, the A340 could climb to efficient cruise altitudes more quickly and fly farther with the CFM56s.

IAE's problem centered on the fact that no more than 27,500 lbs. of thrust could be coaxed out of the engine. The A340 required a minimum of 30,000 lbs. from each engine, with higher required thrust ratings in the future. IAE's only alternative, besides designing a new engine, was to increase the size of the fan and low-pressure turbine. Even this was a costly and time-consuming proposition.

Being the lead engine on the A340 program was extremely lucrative for IAE. Research continued throughout 1986 on a 30,000 lb. thrust V2500 derivative. Partners Pratt & Whitney and Rolls Royce had independently come to the conclusion that a geared, front-fan configuration could deliver the required thrust.

This "SuperFan" engine utilized the V2500 as a basic core but added an ultra-high bypass fan section. This was driven by the augmented low-pressure turbine via a 3:1 gearbox. The variable pitch fan measured

CLIMB - 250KT/300KT/M.78

MAX. CLIMB THRUST	ISA + 15	FROM BRAKE RELEASE	
NORMAL AIR CONDITIONING	CG = 30.0%	TIME (MIN)	FUEL (KG)
ANTI-ICING OFF		DISTANCE (NM)	TAS (KT)

WEIGHT AT BRAKE RELEASE (1000KG)

FL	130	140	150	160	170	180	190
410	19 3408	21 3738	23 4107	26 4529	29 5036	34 5718	
	123 396	137 398	153 400	172 403	197 406	234 411	
390	17 3222	18 3517	20 3838	22 4192	25 4588	27 5046	31 5597
	109 388	120 390	132 392	146 394	163 396	182 399	207 402
370	15 3057	17 3327	18 3616	20 3929	22 4272	24 4652	26 5080
	97 381	107 383	117 384	128 386	141 387	155 389	172 392
350	14 2911	15 3161	17 3428	18 3714	20 4023	22 4361	23 4733
	88 374	96 376	105 377	115 378	125 380	137 381	150 383
330	13 2773	14 3008	15 3257	17 3521	18 3806	20 4113	21 4448
	80 367	88 368	95 370	104 371	113 372	123 373	133 375
310	12 2637	13 2857	14 3090	15 3336	17 3599	18 3881	20 4187
	73 359	79 360	86 362	94 363	102 364	110 365	119 366
290	11 2491	12 2697	13 2913	14 3142	15 3384	17 3644	18 3924
	65 349	71 351	77 352	84 353	91 354	98 355	106 356
270	10 2310	11 2497	12 2694	13 2902	14 3123	15 3357	16 3607
	57 337	62 338	67 339	72 340	78 341	84 341	91 342
250	9 2141	10 2311	11 2492	11 2681	12 2882	13 3095	14 3321
	49 324	54 325	58 326	63 327	68 328	73 329	78 329
240	9 2060	9 2223	10 2395	11 2577	12 2768	13 2971	14 3187
	46 318	50 319	54 320	58 321	63 322	68 323	73 323
220	8 1906	8 2055	9 2212	10 2377	11 2552	11 2737	12 2934
	40 306	43 307	47 308	51 309	55 310	59 310	63 311
200	7 1759	8 1894	8 2037	9 2188	10 2348	10 2517	11 2696
	35 294	38 296	41 296	44 297	47 298	51 299	55 299
180	6 1617	7 1739	7 1869	8 2006	9 2152	9 2306	10 2470
	30 283	33 284	35 285	38 285	41 286	44 287	47 287
160	6 1478	6 1588	7 1705	7 1829	8 1961	8 2100	9 2249
	26 270	28 271	30 272	33 273	35 274	38 274	40 275
140	5 1341	6 1438	6 1543	6 1654	7 1772	7 1898	8 2032
	22 257	24 258	26 259	27 259	30 260	32 261	34 261
120	5 1205	5 1291	5 1383	6 1481	6 1586	6 1699	7 1819
	18 242	20 243	21 244	23 244	25 245	26 246	28 247
100	4 981	4 1047	4 1119	4 1197	5 1280	5 1370	5 1467
	13 215	14 215	15 216	16 217	17 218	18 219	20 219
50	2 671	2 710	3 754	3 802	3 855	3 912	3 975
	7 178	7 178	8 178	8 178	9 179	10 180	10 181
15	2 453	2 473	2 497	2 525	2 557	2 593	2 633
	3 131	3 129	4 128	4 128	4 127	4 128	5 129

PACK FLOW LO	PACK FLOW HI OR/ AND CARGO COOL ON	ENGINE ANTI ICE ON	TOTAL ANTI ICE ON
Δ FUEL = − 1 %	ΔFUEL = + 1 %	Δ FUEL = + 5 %	ΔFUEL = + 8 %

10B -08F0A340-211/-212 CFM56-5C2 21100000C5KG300 0 018590 0 0 2 1.0 500.0 100.00 1 03250.000300.000 .780 15 FCOM-F0-03-05-10-007-15C

Performance data from the Flight Crew Operating Manual (FCOM) Volume 1. (Airbus)

110 in. in diameter; 47 inches larger than a stock V2500. IAE believed the SuperFan could be tested and certified by April of 1991, the same month Airbus planned to fly the A340. To say that hopes were high at IAE, Airbus, and the customer airlines would be an understatement.

IAE released schedules and claims were published regarding weights, costs, and performance of the new powerplant. Airbus managers were briefed by IAE executives just before Christmas of 1986, generating considerable excitement among the A340 crowd. Airbus was satisfied that the proposed engine was technically achievable. Basic figures indicated a takeoff thrust rating of 30,000 lbs. and a specific fuel consumption 15% less than the early V2500s. Even the increased size of the engine's fan diameter would not require lengthening the main landing gear to maintain ground clearance.

With these performance numbers in hand, Airbus Executive Vice President Heribert Flosdorff defined Airbus' position against competing aircraft designs. "Our A330 and A340 products give the airlines the chance for a greater profit potential over a mix of operations; more than a single design could achieve." Aimed directly at McDonnell Douglas, Flosdorff stated, "Performance-wise, we are able to beat the two MD-11 versions Douglas has offered." Even though the V2500 SuperFan was listed as the lead engine for the A340, Airbus made an intelligent decision to provide interested airlines with information and performance numbers for both IAE SuperFan and a version with higher thrust CFM56 models.

Expectations for the new engine within Airbus and IAE were high. As both parties developed their projects further, IAE began to find the promises they had made might not be achievable within the specified time and cost constraints. In short, the entire SuperFan program engine fell apart. IAE backed out of the project for the time being, and under-mined its industry standing along with the industry confidence it had built. Lufthansa's Reinhardt Abraham had negotiated with IAE for engines to power his company's A340s. "I assumed I could rely on their information, as I had in the past when I worked individually with its members. I took it for granted that when they told us about performance and scheduling that we could count on their information. I cannot be sure any more of what they are promising," he said.

When the SuperFan program unraveled, many had wrongly assumed the key to building the A340 lay with the new engine. Although not by its own doing, Airbus had been put on the spot, and the situation handed McDonnell Douglas an opportunity to publicly flog the A340. Douglas President James Worsham made several remarks inferring the A340 was not a true MD-11 competitor. In truth, as history has borne out, the A340 could stand on its own, even with CFM56 power.

Some good did come from the SuperFan debacle. The engineering teams at Airbus were determined not to be thwarted, and worked around the clock to ensure the original A340 design goals were met. CFM saved the day with an uprated version of the CFM56. With an extension to the wingspan, an increase in fuel capacity, and a higher gross weight, the original performance numbers were achieved and even exceeded, even though the aircraft was slightly larger.

Prior to the SuperFan situation, CFM had proved to Airbus management how much CFM wanted to be the engine of choice for the A340. CFM executives signed a Memo of Understanding to develop a CFM56 derivative capable of producing 28,600 lbs. of thrust. But with all the attention on IAE and the SuperFan, nothing came of it at that time.

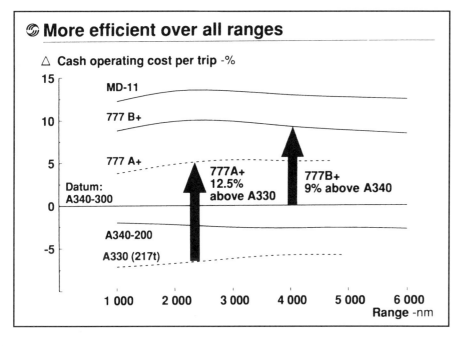

Airbus marketing material that shows operating costs in relation to aircraft range. The use of four engines, according to Airbus, means lower actual costs on longer routes. (Airbus)

The CFM56-5C2 was mounted on General Electric's Boeing 707 test bed at the Mojave, California facility. The fan's bypass air is mixed with the core air at the exit, leaving an aerodynamically clean nacelle. Seen here on a prototype A340, the cowling allows easy access for maintenance. (Airbus)

CFM kept developing the -56 series, coaxing up to 30,600 lbs. of thrust from the re-fanned -5C1. This new thrust rating was achieved with an impressive four percent lower fuel burn than the -5A1 model, as used on the A320. Even though a develop-ment version of the -5C1 had been run in November of 1986, CFM was unwilling to commit formally to this thrust rating. After the SuperFan situation, CFM wanted to be absolutely positive it could provide the required thrust with reliability. Six months later, testing had shown the -5C1 would live up to the task. Airbus and CFM signed an exclusive agreement on April 8, 1987.

The -5 engine allowed Airbus to use cowlings and blocker thrust reverse doors similar to those on

The CFM56-5C4 provides 34,000 lbs. of thrust on a standard, sea level day. For anti-icing, hot engine bleed air is ducted into the natural metal leading edge of the inlet. The vents appearing on the engine pylon are exhaust vents for the oil cooler.
(Scott E. Germain)

CFM56-5A powered A320, cutting the time required to design and test those components. Installed weight of the CFM56-5C1 turned out to be one ton lighter than the SuperFan would have been, reducing airframe weight by 8,820 pounds. This allowed Airbus to rework the payload and range figures of the A340 to higher values. Two-thousand pounds of additional structure were added, with a net weight savings of 6,820 lbs.

Final Changes

Wind tunnel testing at British Aerospace and DaimlerChrysler led to several final changes on the A340 wing. Span was increased by another 4 ft. 3 in. for a total of 192 ft., 5 in. Winglets, canted outward and measuring 9 ft. 6 in., were also added to the wingtips. Effectively increasing wingspan at all altitudes, these surfaces also cut drag by weakening the wingtip vortices.

Finally, small portions of some secondary wing structure metallurgy were altered to include a very small amount of aluminum-lithium alloy

The nine-foot six-inch winglets were added to cut drag and increase efficiency. Each inner and outer aileron contains two actuators for redundancy. The third flap fairing from the tip contains a fuel jettison pipe at its end. Dual position lights and a strobe light are located within the clear cover on the wing tip.
(Scott E. Germain)

Airbus originally thought the -200 would sell equally as well as the -300, but the reverse has proven true. Austrian Airlines' A340-200 OE-LAG A340 is pictured over the Pyrenees on a systems proving flight. (Airbus)

content. The sum of these changes, and the switch to the CFM56 engines, allowed the A340 to grow from a 524,700 lb. aircraft to a 542,300 lb. aircraft at takeoff. Although maximum payload was unchanged, takeoff and landing performance had been improved.

Two models of the A340 were available at program launch, the -200 and the stretched -300. With the CFM56-5C1 engines, these aircraft generated a seat-mile cost 12% lower than the competitor's three- and four-engined airplanes on 4,000+ nautical mile routes. Over the MD-11, the airlines were forecast to see an approximate savings of $2 million dollars per aircraft per year. Airbus was marketing the A340 on several fronts, including its primary strengths of advanced technology, lower operating costs, and fleet commonality. The competing MD-11, although introduced to the mar-

ket earlier, was being plagued with service difficulties, performance problems, and lackluster sales.

Considered the base version, the A340-200 offered a fuselage 12 frames longer than its A300-600 cousin. The A340-300 featured an additional eight fuselage frames to bring the length to 208 feet, 8 inches. As with previous Airbus aircraft, much of the fuselage would be produced in Germany by Daimler-Chrysler. The aluminum fuselage components feature advanced single-piece light alloy castings, and access panels made with Super Plastic Forming/Diffusion Bonded titanium techniques.

Official Program Launch

The executives of the Airbus supervisory board beamed with pride on June 5, 1987, when they gave the green light to publicly announce the

A330/340 program. After 17 years, Roger Beteille and Henri Ziegler's dream of producing a world-class, long-range wide-body had finally been realized. One week later, the Paris Air Show served as the venue for the official launch of the program. The air show gave Airbus a full-press, home-field advantage to market their new wide-body aircraft.

The details of the production and test program revealed specific market changes had recently occurred. Worldwide transportation requirements had created a higher than anticipated demand in the four-engine, long-range market. At the time, Airbus had planned on developing the twin-engine A330 first to fill a market perceived as more urgent. With the market shift towards a four-engine aircraft, Airbus simply changed their focus on developing the A340 first. This was an easy task because the A330/A340

pallet station to be converted to passenger seats. The kits would change the seating capacity to 231 passengers and room for four pallets in a manner of minutes, and a passenger-only configuration could also be created. Zero Fuel Weight for the Combi was raised to 385,800 lbs., and the landing weight was increased by 6,614 lbs. to 403,400 lbs.

No customers opted for the A340 Combi, possibly as a result of a serious accident involving a Boeing 747

Air cargo has increasingly become more important to airlines, and the A340 is equipped to handle the demand. Loading and unloading of pallet or LD cargo containers is made quick and easy with motorized ground equipment shown here. (Airbus)

was always viewed as a single program, and the two aircraft were virtually identical.

During this period, an almost uncontrollable demand for air cargo became readily apparent; huge profits were being generated by what was carried below the cabin floor as well as above it. Airbus took advantage of the A340's flexibility and quickly developed the A340-300 Combi. The dual-role Combi marked the first time a new aircraft had this option from the beginning of the program.

The Combi differed from the passenger version by adding a 101 in. by 134 in. cargo door in the left rear fuselage. The rear cabin floor, where it normally slopes up towards the tail, was also flattened. Accommodations in the Combi supported 201 passengers in three classes, and room for six standard 96 in. by 125 in. cargo pallets.

Airbus also proposed quick-change kits that would allow each

Combi. The accident generated design and safety concerns, along with more stringent rules for certification. With no takers, Airbus dropped the variant from the product list.

Crew Rest Facilities

It was apparent that flights lasting 12 to 14 hours would require additional crew members and rest facilities to be incorporated into the aircraft. As with earlier Lockheed Constellations, Douglas DC-7s and Boeing Stratocruisers, Airbus offered the A340 with optional crew rest facilities.

For the cockpit crew, an area immediately behind the flight deck could be equipped with 75 in. top and bottom bunks. Depending on the layout selected, the bottom bunk could be converted into two seats, while the top bunk folds up and away to provide room. Amenities include crew baggage stowage, an entertainment center, fresh air vents, reading lights, and emergency oxygen dispensers. A sliding panel allows an immediate view of the cockpit.

Another crew rest area, called a Lower Deck Crew Rest Compartment (LDCRC), can be loaded in the forward position of the aft cargo bay. Roughly the size of two LD3 cargo containers, the LDCRC is also equipped with connections for entertainment, environmental, oxygen, and lighting services. Accessed via a door from the passenger cabin, a wide staircase leads down to the rest area. Up to seven bunks, a changing room, a refrigerator, and an intercom between the cockpit and cabin attendant panels are built in to the module. The LDCRC must be unoccupied during takeoff and landing.

Most airlines have ordered the LDCRC's for crew use, and have expressed interest in offering similar facilities to premium-fare passen-

The LDCRC can be quickly loaded into the rear cargo bay of the A340. Connections for electrical, pneumatic, and communications are provided. (Airbus)

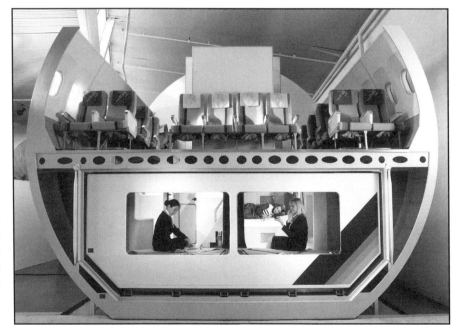

Shown in mockup form, the refined Lower Deck Crew Rest Container (LDCRC) facility provides crew members with a roomy below-deck area for sleep or relaxation during long flights. The LDCRC occupies the forward cargo slot behind the wing, thereby not compromising revenue generating area in the cabin. Most airlines have ordered this option. (Airbus)

A mockup of the underfloor crew rest area, showing the amount of space available. Each bunk is equipped with reading lights, a clock with alarm, and environmental controls. (Airbus)

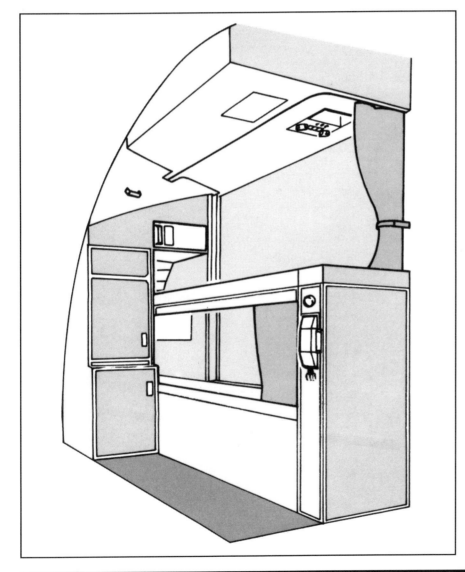

gers. The new concept, to be available on future A340-500 and -600 versions, would entail lowering the cargo deck floor for additional room. Travelers could use these personal berths as offices to conduct business, or to sleep and reduce the effects of jet lag. Other ideas include personal service salons or meeting facilities.

Moving Towards Production

Using 1987 currency values, Airbus Industrie's Chairman J. F. Strauss quoted the A340 price at $84 million dollars, while the A330 came to $80 million per copy. Upon rollout four years later, an Associated Press article would put a $104 million dollar price tag on each A340. Compared with the $135 million dollar 747, the A340 appeared to be a very good bargain. Airbus salesmen were quick to point out Boeing had enjoyed a monopoly in this market, and could set the 747 price higher than a competitive market would allow. Furthermore, as Airbus liked to point out, the direct operating costs for the A340 came in a good deal lower than the three- and four-engine competitors.

Interested airlines were provided with detailed performance and economic information so they could assess how the A340 might fit into their fleets. Lufthansa had the distinction of being the launch customer for the A340, signing an agreement with Airbus for 15 firm orders and an option on 15 more. Split between the

The A340 can be ordered with a flight crew rest area directly behind the cockpit. A partition can be opened to allow the captain to directly view the flight deck at any time. Two bunks, storage lockers, and reading lights are built in. (Airbus)

-200 and -300 versions, the A340 would join A300, A310, and A320 types already in service.

Lufthansa considered the A340 definition very satisfactory. After entry to service, calculations would be made by the airline – not the manufacturer – that would show nine percent better operating economics with the A340. Since Lufthansa already operated a significant fleet of DC-10s, one would think the MD-11 would have been a logical replacement. The decision to acquire the A340 over the MD-11 spoke volumes about the attention to detail Airbus applied to the A340 and the level of efficiency it possessed.

Lufthansa received its first A340 in January, 1993, and began service two months later on March 15. Lufthansa is currently the largest A340 operator with a mixed fleet of 17 -200 and -300 aircraft. Future orders for advanced A340 versions and additional 200/300 versions were placed. Air France was also a launch customer, signing orders for 16 aircraft.

In all, the A330/340 program had garnered 157 orders from thirteen different operators including TWA, Sabena, Thai International, and TAP Air Portugal. Northwest Airlines also signed an order on February 10, 1989, a week before Lufthansa did. The twenty aircraft order would have made the carrier the first North American operator of the A340. However, financial problems within the airline forced the conversion of the order to A330s for delivery at a later date.

Currently the only airline based in North America to operate the A340, Air Canada signed on for nine A340-300s to add to its fleet of 65 A319s and A320s. Once an airline that operated aircraft manufactured solely in the United States, the Canadian carrier is a prime example of the Airbus Cross Crew Qualification (CCQ) concept. Flight crews can fly trip pairings in any of the three Airbus types they operate. Future orders were also placed for seven additional A340s, making Air Canada one of the consortium's best customers. Next-

generation A340-500s and -600s will join the fleet after 2002.

While orders for the A340 did not exactly pour in, they built up well with additional orders from Cathay Pacific, Singapore, Turkish, and Air Mauritius. British carrier Virgin Atlantic also bought the A340, allowing service to expand to the American west coast, the Asia-Pacific region, and South Africa. With a cabin that matched the seat-demand on the routes, it appeared Airbus marketing strategy hit the nail on the head. Virgin Chairman Richard Branson stated, "We like the A340's size, economics, and unrestricted range. We're proud to be buying European." Virgin orders included the second and third A340-300s used in the development portion of the flight test program.

The Production Line

Laying the manufacturing groundwork for the A340 was a complex task spread over several continents. As with other Airbus

German flag carrier Lufthansa has the distinction of being the world's largest operator of Airbus equipment. D-AJGB is shown here on approach to Frankfurt. (Karl Cornil)

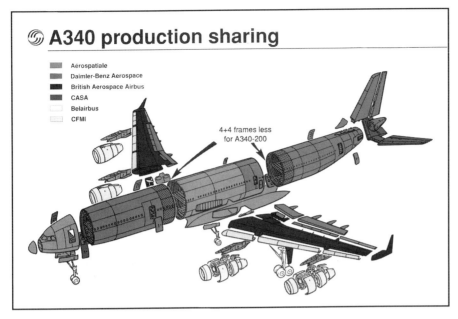

A340 production sharing

- Aérospatiale
- Daimler-Benz Aerospace
- British Aerospace Airbus
- CASA
- Belairbus
- CFMI

4+4 frames less
for A340-200

A340 production sharing between Airbus partners. (Airbus)

products, certain components were built at each partner's production facility with subsequent transport to the Clément Ader facility in Toulouse, France. Final assembly would then take place, with painting, furnishing, testing, and delivery occurring soon after.

Building an aircraft the size of the A340 would be a challenging task even if a central manufacturing plant were used. What makes the process almost seamless is Computer Aided Design/Manufacturing (CAD/CAM) systems used by each partner. Designed solely on computer, the A330/A340 are the first airliners to be 100% "paperless" aircraft. This meant the fit tolerances of compo-

An aerial view of the Clément Ader facility in full swing. Built in under two years, the facility is dedicated to A330/340 production. Designed around the modular assembly concept, the innovative and time-saving method does away with linear production lines and the need to stock costly inventory. (Airbus)

AIRLINERTECH
SERIES

nents made on different continents by different manufacturers would be a non-issue, even on the first aircraft. Digital data could also be transferred easily between facilities.

DaimlerChrysler builds a significant portion of the fuselage sections, the vertical tail, rudder, tail cone, flaps, and flap fairings. When the wing boxes arrive from Chester, the leading and trailing edge devices, along with the spoilers, are attached.

British Aerospace builds the basic wing structure at its Broughton facility, then transports them to the DaimlerChrysler plant in Bremen, Germany, to be fitted with hydraulic, electrical, and pneumatic components, flaps, and lateral controls. Belairbus manufactures the leading edge slats, which are also installed in Germany. Each A340 wing contains three times the work content required on the smaller A320 wing.

A key part of the A340 production program relies on the A300-600 Super Transporter aircraft, commonly referred to as the "Beluga." The purpose-built Beluga fulfills the requirement for a large capacity aircraft capable of transporting oversized aircraft components. Replacing the old turbo-prop Super Guppies, the cavernous Beluga allows a complete pair of A340 wings to be easily transported between production plants.

Spain's CASA is responsible for making the horizontal stabilizers, elevators, nose landing gear doors, and the forward cabin entry doors.

French partner Aerospatiale builds the cockpit and forward fuse-

The sun catches an Air Canada A340-300 (C-FYLC) as it begins its taxi to the active. Air Canada is the only North America-based A340 operator, but is one of Airbus' best customers. The A340s work alongside the smaller A319s and A320 cousins. (Karl Cornil)

A340 launch customer Air France signed on early to the A340 program. The A340-300's range of 7,300 nm and an extremely comfortable cabin make the aircraft a favorite with passengers and flight crew alike. (Airbus)

Commonality is key. Cathay Pacific operates both the A330 and A340, and realizes the benefits of Airbus' Cross Crew Qualification (CCQ) program. (Airbus)

As one of the prototype A340s receives maintenance in the background, No. 12's wing and center section is mated to the fore and aft fuselage. Due to the use of computer aided design and manufacturing, the fit of components built in different factories in different countries is exceptional. (Airbus)

British Aerospace produces the wing boxes for all Airbus designs, including the A340 series. The box structures are 98 feet long, the largest ever manufactured in Europe. Additional items, including flaps, slats, and their associated tracks, will be installed in Bremen, Germany. The first set is prepared for shipment during July 1990. (Airbus)

lage sections, selected center fuselage and wing box sections, and the engine mounting pylons. Final assembly and cabin interior fitting also occurs at the Toulouse facility adjacent to the Blagnac Airport. Each component – be it a wing, fuselage section, or cockpit cab – is completed right down to wiring, cannon plugs, and attach fittings. This "plug and play" process is a first in aircraft manufacturing on this scale, and provides Airbus with an extremely tight and efficient manufacturing schedule.

The final assembly process is a marvel in planning and synchronization. Production schedules are sequenced so components arrive for final assembly as they are needed. Components delivered to Toulouse are given 24 hours to acclimate to the local climate before being assembled

with other components. Little time is wasted with storing components in inventory or having too much of part A when part B is needed.

Production efficiency is enhanced by the use of automation on several Airbus production lines. For the first time in airliner production, robots are used to drill holes and install fasteners within the aircraft structure. Intended to compliment – not replace – humans on the production line, the automated robots perform over 13,000 operations on each aircraft. Automatic drilling machines, rivet machines, and a 283 foot long routing machine help achieve high levels of precision and uniformity throughout component construction. Robotics are also used to join the front, center, and rear fuselage sections in Toulouse.

For a decidedly European company, Airbus has a surprising impact on the aerospace industry in the United States as well. Approximately thirty-five percent of the components used in Airbus aircraft are made in America, and every transport that Airbus builds brings equal returns to both the American and European economies. General Electric, Pratt and Whitney, Allied-Signal, B.F. Goodrich, Honeywell, Rockwell Collins, Sundstrand, Rohr, and Westinghouse all contribute various parts, engines, and assemblies to the A340 program.

Worldwide, Airbus has more than 1,500 suppliers representing 27 countries. In the United States alone, 800 suppliers make parts or components for Airbus aircraft and generate an annual revenue of $5 billion dollars. Components produced by Asian aerospace companies include structural parts, thrust reverser doors, and landing gear jacks. Australian contributions include main landing gear bay structures and doors. Cooperative agreements exist

A static test airframe component is loaded into Super Guppy #4 in Toulouse, France. Testing was performed at the Centre d'Essais Aeronautique de Toulouse (CEAT) in the summer of 1991, and verified the structure met design specifications. (Airbus)

Structural assembly of the fuselage shells taking place in Hamburg, Germany. Fuselage skins are laid over formers and stringers, then riveted in place. (Airbus)

with companies in 19 additional countries, with an estimated 100,000 people involved with the production of Airbus aircraft around the world.

The A300-600ST, called the "Beluga," was an in-house answer to the aging and slow Super Guppy turboprops. Four Super Transporters have been built with a fifth on the way. These aircraft are key to the modular production process Airbus pioneered. (Airbus)

Specialized platforms allow easy loading of A340 components into the hold of the Belugas. Notice the flap and the parts bins loaded next to the fuselage section. (Airbus)

Roll Out and First Flight

The first A340, a -300 minus engines and interior, was rolled out by Aerospatiale in Toulouse on March 8, 1991. By this time, the A340 was competing with the MD-11 as well as Boeing's 777. The new Boeing, heralded as a new-generation, long-range twin, was capable of carrying 330 passengers in a three-class cabin. It featured a Fly By Wire flight control system, but lacked the protections built into the A340's FBW system.

In Toulouse, the number one A340 was undergoing initial functional testing, including the first power-up of its electrical system. The completion of the airframe and initial testing validated the technologies Airbus had selected for the aircraft, as well as the CAD/CAM system and modular assembly process. Even for a prototype, the first-time fit of parts and components was impressive.

Daniel Huet, the A340 production director for Aerospatiale, expressed his ideas on the production process. "Obviously, the assembly of only the number one aircraft does not give us a sufficient statistical base to draw too many conclusions from. But, we have seen that the productivity level is up to our expectations." Particular concern lay with the joining of the wing and fuselage. "I have to admit," Huet said, "that we were a bit worried about the computer-controlled robots that perform the circumferential riveting. As it turns out, we were really pleased with how things turned out with the number one aircraft."

Static fuel tests, along with vibration testing and painting soon followed. As the first A340 passed through the initial test phases, designers were working on a weight reduction program. As with any new design, weight creeps higher as changes are made. Airbus planned on having the number three test aircraft, and one that would be the first delivered to a customer, to come in on target.

The official roll-out ceremony occurred on October 4, 1991 in front of 6,000 guests from the aerospace industry, airlines, and the press. Registered as F-WWAI, the aircraft made its first flight a few weeks later on October 25. The four hour and forty-seven minute flight was made by Captain Pierre Baud, First Officer Nick Warner, and Flight Test Engi-

The first A340 is seen upon completion in Toulouse, France. Taken before painting and the official unveiling, the aircraft sits complete with winglets, fairings, and engines. First flight took place on October 25, 1991. (Airbus)

As of March 1992, A340 production rate was running at two aircraft per month. By 1994, the goal of seven aircraft per month had been achieved. The third aircraft is shown here in the final assembly bay, already having its systems tested and engines hung. (Airbus)

neers Jean-Marie Mathios and Jurgen Hammer, and Flight Test Development Director Gerard Guyout. The crew reported excellent basic handling qualities and no major problems.

Flight Test

Flight test proved to be extremely productive, thanks to the dedicated SPATIAAL flight test computer and real-time telemetry. The SPATI-AAL system allowed the flight test engineer, stationed in the cabin of the aircraft, to load and investigate different control law combinations while airborne. With this capability, the test pilots could consecutively evaluate several software combina-

tions and decide which produced acceptable results. This method saved a lot of time as the aircraft did not have to land, be reconfigured or re-rigged, and take off again.

By the end of 1991, over 100 hours had been flown and the program was ahead of schedule. A second aircraft joined the program on February 3, 1992, and Airbus was shooting for certification by the end of the year. With no schedule slippages, deliveries to the airlines would begin by early 1993.

The initial test program included handling at all slat and flap settings, and determination of the best settings for takeoff and landing. Stalls in different configurations were investigated, and Angle of Attack

protection was also evaluated. Minimum unstick speed was established, as well as flight envelope expansion to 40,000 feet and Mach .85. Autopilot functions were proven, and automatic landings were made in low visibility conditions. Flutter testing revealed information that would help future versions of the A340 take to the skies with higher capacities and heavier gross weights.

As the speed envelope was widened, flight test found a buffet problem while accelerating through .83 Mach. Studying the airflow in a wind tunnel, engineers saw flow separation on the wing outboard of the number one and number four engines. A small blister was added to modify the flow beneath the wing,

F-WWAS hits the troughs during water-ingestion testing at Bretigny, France. Testing occurred with all slat and flaps set to ensure water would not enter the engine intakes and cause a flameout. Notice the forward angle of the water rising ahead of the main wheels. (Airbus)

and the chord of the number one slat was increased. These changes also resulted in a 1.5% drag reduction. Subsequent production aircraft were remedied by changing the washout of the wing and by making slight modifications to the engine pylon/wing junction.

With only 200 hours of flight time, Airbus demonstrated the abilities of the A340 on a series of flights to and from the Asian Aerospace Show in February. Three flights were made, the first from Toulouse direct to Singapore. Flown in 12 hours 55 minutes, the A340 arrived in excellent mechanical shape, and could have been readied for depar-

ture in about an hour. At the conclusion of the show a week later, the A340 was flown 7 hours 15 minutes to Mauritius and refueled. That same day, the aircraft launched for Toulouse, arriving there 13 hours 50 minutes later. The flight time included a one hour airborne hold due to

The A340 was introduced to the world on October 4, 1991, at the Toulouse, France facility. Attended by over 5,500 people, the lavish ceremony marked the public debut of the world's longest ranged airliner, and the largest aircraft built to date by the European consortium. From bases such as Frankfurt, London, Paris, and Hong Kong, the A340 put many worldwide destinations within direct, unrefueled reach. (Airbus)

Airbus Industrie was the first manufacturer to demonstrate automatic landings in the southern hemisphere using satellite-based navigation. Performed in August 1995 in Mauritius and Mmabatho, South Africa, the 100 meter enroute navigation accuracy was increased to 2 meters by an additional ground station set up by the runway. The station comprises a small circular antenna, two electronics boxes, and a VHF antenna to transmit data to the aircraft. (Airbus)

fog. The "Singapore Fling" highlighted the A340's long range, a high level of system reliability, and the overall capability of the aircraft.

In all, six A340s were used in the flight test program. Because of market demands and orders made by the airlines, the A340-300 would be the first to enter service, followed closely by the -200.

Throughout every test flight in the A340 program, the flight test engineers in the cabin had the ability to see and record the data being generated by the flight. Real-time data

V_{MU} – minimum unstick speed – testing was completed in January 1992 in Toulouse. The trials measure the lowest speed that the aircraft will take off at various weights and CG locations. Nose attitudes are typically high during these tests, as shown here. A skid protects the fuselage from damage. (Airbus)

transmission also took place via a ground station and a satellite link to the Flight Test Control Center back in Toulouse. The area used for test covered airspace from the English Channel to the Spanish border, and along the Pyrenees to the Mediterranean coast. The area also reaches well into the Atlantic Upper Information Region and is covered wholly by French air traffic control. When test aircraft are airborne, a single controller is responsible for working that flight.

Telemetry had been used for years in flight test, but was considered a recording device if the aircraft was lost. Airbus, during the A320 program, had begun to use telemetry as an everyday tool to begin processing data even before the aircraft had landed. During the A340 program, the data was downlinked via satellite to a mini control center for immediate processing. On test flights lasting five hours, this invaluable tool saved time in processing the thousands of data points being generated.

Toulouse-based engineers could monitor the "hot" data, and had the ability to ask the flight crew to modify a procedure, or re-fly a test point if the data appeared invalid. This interaction between the flight and ground teams considerably improved the quality of data from each A340 test, and contributed to the overall quickness of the program.

By the summer of 1992, the A340 test program had come up to full speed. Previous test cards had verified the designer's calculations, and flights were now focused on demonstrating the aircraft to certification authorities. Early reports from

Water tanks were used to change the aircraft weight and center of gravity during test flights. Tanks were also installed on the lower deck floor. (Airbus)

The flight deck crew of the first A340 flight included Captain Pierre Baud (left) and First Officer Nick Warner. Baud was Vice President Flight Division and Chief Test Pilot. (Airbus)

The A330/340 flight test fleet appears in one place at one time. The distinctive Airbus Prototype paint scheme compliments the modern lines of the aircraft and generates an easy identifiable image for Airbus. (Airbus)

Prototype A340s were fitted with an extensive suite of flight test instruments and telemetry systems. Thousands of parameters were satellite-linked to the Toulouse Flight Test Center. Housed inside the fuselage, this test rig gives an idea of the complexity of the system. (Airbus)

customer airline pilots and aerospace journal writers extolled the virtues of the aircraft, citing its comfort and how easy it was to fly. Testing continued, with hot and high airfield performance taking place during July in Saudi Arabia, and cold weather testing taking place in Kiruna, Sweden and Yakutsk, Siberia that December.

The final phase of flight test centered on route-proving, with demonstrations showing the A340 was worthy of commercial airline service. From Frankfurt, two A340s made medium- and long-range flights across the globe to destinations such as Fairbanks, Perth, Honolulu, La Paz, and many more. Commercial routes were tested over a span of 280 flight hours with airline

Hot weather climate testing occurred at Lhasa airport, elevation 11,713 feet. The A340 passed the test with high marks, even demonstrating the ability to make a three-engine ferry flight. (Airbus)

Cold weather trials underway in Kiruna, Sweden. The aircraft had to demonstrate operations in all climate extremes. (Airbus)

Calibration markings appear on the left wing and winglet as an A340-300 prototype flies a test card over the Pyrenees. Airbus has use of extremely large quantities of airspace to conduct test operations, and the use of dedicated air traffic controllers for each flight. (Airbus)

The first commercial A340 was delivered to Lufthansa, an airline that operates almost every type of Airbus. D-AIBD, one of the original A340-200s ordered, is shown about to land at Frankfurt. (Brian Stevenson)

Air France closely followed Lufthansa in being an initial operator of the A340. The French carrier leased an additional five A340s from Sabena when that airline opted not to take delivery. (Karl Cornil)

style intensity. Ground personnel were also able to observe ground handling procedures at outstations, and airline officials, travel agents, and press members were introduced to the aircraft.

Certification and Service

Fourteen months and over 2,400 hours of flight testing paid off on December 22, 1992 when the European Joint Aviation Authority (JAA) awarded the A340 its type certificate. The A340 program marked the first time the 18 nation Joint Authorities had certificated a new airliner, and the first time simultaneous approval was granted for two versions of a single aircraft. The American Federal Aviation Administration (FAA) approved the A340 the following February.

The first commercial A340-200 was delivered to Deutsche Lufthansa on January 19, 1992. At a ceremony in Frankfurt, Lufthansa Chairman Jurgen Weber stated, "We are proud of our leading role in the A340 and look forward to the important savings it will bring in fuel consumption, noise, and emissions." Lufthansa also went on record as saying the A340's introduction to service was the smoothest ever of a new aircraft to its fleet.

Air France was also gearing up for A340 service, with crews beginning flight training in the last week of February. Regular trans-Atlantic service would begin in mid-March after the necessary flight and ground crews had been trained and approved by the JAA/FAA.

INSIDE THE AIRBUS A340

The fuselage cross section of the A340 is based on the A310 design, with a different center section to accommodate the new wing and attach points. The "short body" A340-200 measures 194 ft. 10 in. long, while the -300 is eight frames longer for a total length of 208 ft. 11 in. Height to the tip of the tail is 54 ft. 11 in. Both versions have the same wing, spanning 197 ft. 10 in.

The wing itself is a three-spar box design incorporating aluminum construction. Some secondary structure is fashioned from aluminum lithium, and aluminum alloys are used in many of the fittings. The outboard flaps, flap track fairings, ailerons, spoilers, and leading/ trailing edge fixed surfaces utilize carbon, graphite, and other composites in their construction. A total of 13% of the wing structure, by weight, is made up of composite materials. Early winglets were carbon fiber, but are now made from aluminum alloy.

The vertical stabilizer design was also borrowed from the A310, while new horizontal tail surfaces were designed to incorporate a trim fuel tank. The outer main box is constructed from graphite epoxy with an aluminum alloy center section.

Engines

Four CFM-56-5C high-bypass turbofans power the A340-200 and -300 variants. Three different versions of the engine have been used; from the early 31,200 lb. thrust -5C2 and 32,500 lb. thrust -5C3 to the current 34,000 lb. thrust -5C4.

The CFM56 has proven itself as a reliable, efficient, and easy engine to operate. Used on many different commercial aircraft, the engines feature a 6.6:1 bypass ratio and relatively low noise emissions. Each engine weighs 5,494 lbs. and can process 1,027 lbs. of air per second. After the front fan, four low-pressure and nine high-pressure compressors feed the annular combustion chambers. Twenty fuel nozzles and two separate ignition systems provide the fire.

An accessory case, driven by a shaft from the engine gearbox, houses the Integrated Drive Generator (IDG), hydraulic pump, oil pump, engine driven pump, HMU, and the engine's FADEC electrical generator.

Each engine is controlled by a Full Authority Digital Engine Control (FADEC), a computer that completely manages the start and operation of the engine. Each FADEC contains dual-channel redundancy, one being active while the other is in standby. A failure of the active channel automatically transfers control to the other channel. Since FADEC electrical power is supplied by a magnetic alternator, a failure of the aircraft's electrical system will not effect the operation of the engines.

The FADECs control and monitor a plethora of parameters, including thrust management, idle thrust control, acceleration schedule, and movement of the variable stator vanes. Limitation protection, reverse thrust, and data transmission to the

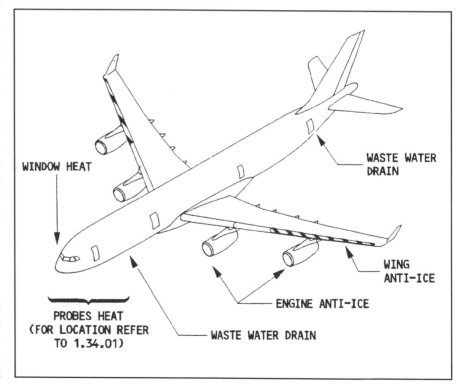

Areas of electrical and pneumatic anti/de-ice protection on the A340. (Airbus)

The vertical tail and rudder of the A340 are the same design as the earlier A310, and provides excellent directional control in the event of two engines failing on the same side. (Scott E. Germain)

The FIRE portion of the overhead panel has fire push buttons that light up red if an engine is on fire. In such cases, the metal safety clip is lifted, allowing the button to be pushed. All fluids to the engine are cut off, and the engine is automatically shut down. The Agent 1 and Agent 2 push buttons discharge extinguishing gas into the engine and cowling. (Scott E. Germain)

aircraft recording system is also handled by the FADECs.

As part of the autoflight system in the A340, the thrust levers are also Fly By Wire, and contain no mechanical linkage to the engines. As a result of this, when the Flight Management and Guidance System (FMGS) commands a change in thrust, the thrust levers do not move. Detents in the thrust lever range include Idle, CL (Max Climb Power), MCT/FLX (Maximum Continuous Thrust/Flex Thrust), and TOGA (Takeoff/Go Around Thrust). Autothrust is automatically armed on takeoff, and becomes active when the thrust levers are brought to the CLB detent after takeoff. If any combinations of engines are inoperative, autothrust remains active with the thrust levers between Idle and MCT/FLX detents.

Pressurization & Air-Conditioning

Air for cabin pressurization and environmental control is provided by engine or APU bleed air. The hot, compressed air passes through a pre-cooler and then flows to the air-conditioning packs in the belly of the aircraft. Cooled further by a heat exchanger and an air cycle machine, the conditioned air is routed to the cockpit and cabin. Cockpit controls and digital readouts allow the flight crew to mix conditioned air and hot bleed air to provide the required temperature. The flight attendants, using controls on their cabin control panels, can further fine-tune the cabin temperature. The air distribution system within the cabin is designed to prevent drafts, and is baffled to cut

A flight attendant uses the Cabin Intercommunication and Data System (CIDS), a computer panel that displays and controls all cabin lighting, signals, and communications. The display on the left shows the status of all cabin doors. (Airbus)

The pressurization systems provide a maximum pressure differential of 8.7 psi, while bleed air and air-conditioning packs provide air to keep the cabin comfortable. Flight attendants can further heat or cool the cabin with controls on their CIDS panel. (Airbus)

down on cabin noise, a point that has earned the A340 the title of the "Quietest Cabin in the Sky."

Dual Cabin Pressurization Controller (CPC) computers provide fully automatic pressurization scheduling. Since the FMGS knows the departure and arrival airports as well as their elevations, the CPCs can import this information and set the pressurization schedule. If this data is not available, the pilots simply select the landing field elevation and the pressurization will continue to operate automatically. Manual control of the system, in case of a dual CPC failure, can be maintained with controls on the overhead CABIN PRESS panel. Maximum cabin differential is 8.7 psi.

Autoflight

The A340 Flight Management and Guidance System (FMGS) is the brain of the aircraft and its autoflight/prediction capabilities. Dual Flight Management and Guidance Computers (FMGC) provide flight and navigation data to the pilots, and perform many traditional pilot functions. The flight crew can interface with the autoflight system two ways – through the Multipurpose Control and Display Units (MCDU) for Managed Guidance, or through the Flight Control Unit (FCU) for Selected Guidance.

Each FMGC has its own database divided into two parts. The first is a non-modifiable database tailored for the customer airline and its area of operations. Standard navigation data, routes, waypoints, airport, and alternate airport data is included, and is updated on a 28-day cycle. The second database is user-modifiable, and allows the pilots to store up to 20 waypoints, ten runways, 20 navaids, and five routes.

The philosophy of automated flight in the A340 revolves around these two types of guidance. Managed guidance occurs when the flight crew gives control of the aircraft to the autoflight system. The aircraft will then fly along a pre-programmed lateral, vertical, and speed profile as entered into the MCDU before the flight. Conversely, Selected Guidance allows the flight crew to immediately select a different airspeed, heading, altitude, or vertical speed target on the FCU, which is centrally located on the cockpit glareshield. Selected Guidance always has priority over Managed Guidance.

During preflight cockpit preparation, the crew enters the departure runway, departure procedure, enroute waypoints, arrival, approach, landing runway, missed approach, and route to the alternate airport. If the route is stored in the aircraft database, route generation is greatly simplified. The FMGCs then generate optimum lateral and vertical flight profiles and predicted progress along the entire flight path. Each MCDU shares information with the other two, and in case of failure, one is sufficient to control the entire system.

Any of the flight plan waypoints can be modified, changed, added, or deleted on the MCDU at any time. Additionally, if air traffic control gives altitude or speed restrictions at a waypoint, they can be entered on the MCDU, and the autoflight system will guide the aircraft to the target. If the aircraft can't physically meet the restriction, a SPEED

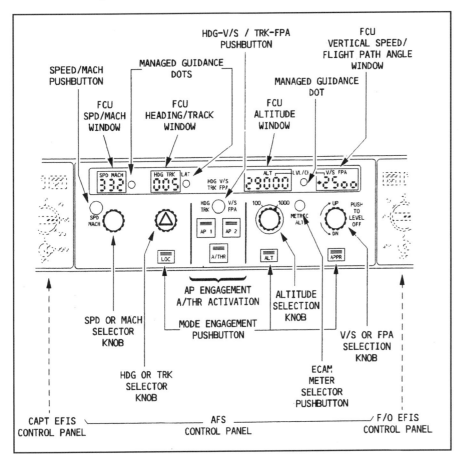

The FCU serves as the short-term interface between the flight crew and the aircraft's FMGS. The airspeed, heading, altitude, and vertical speed knobs can be pushed or pulled to distinguish between Managed or Selected functions. (Airbus)

BRAKE or TOO STEEP PATH message will appear to alert the pilots.

The MCDUs are mounted on the center pedestal and are used continuously during flight. Information is displayed on its cathode ray tube screen, and is capable of 14 text lines and six different colors. Computerized peripherals such as the Centralized Maintenance System (CMS), ARINC communications system, or the ACARS system can be accessed through the MCDU at any time. Each MCDU function is accessed via a function key that allows the pilot to call up the desired page quickly.

DIR calls up the DIRECT TO function, allowing the aircraft to proceed directly from present position to any stored or manually entered waypoint. An Abeam Waypoints function will automatically string the flight plan waypoints along the new direct course line to make fuel and time checks easier.

PROG calls up the Progress Page corresponding to the active phase of flight. Optimum and maximum cruise altitudes are displayed, and entry fields are available to allow the pilot to update the FMGS position and display a distance and bearing to any location.

PERF calls up the Performance pages, which display entry fields for speed/Mach for each phase of flight (Climb, Cruise, Descent, etc.). The Takeoff Performance Page has additional entry fields for V-speeds, Flex takeoff temperature, and Runway Shift, and also displays climb speed for the current weight. The Approach Performance Page has entry fields for destination altimeter setting, landing wind conditions, temperature, and engine-out acceleration altitude.

INIT calls up the Initialization A page for insertion of the route city pair and the flight plan. Inertial reference system alignment is also selected here. INIT B is accessed for insertion of aircraft weight, fuel on board, and center of gravity information.

DATA calls up the Data index page, allowing access to other pages displaying aircraft position, aircraft status, runways, waypoints,

The MCDU is the long-term interface between the flight crew and the Flight Management and Guidance System. The buttons next to the display screen are Line Select Keys, and allow direct insertion of data to the FMGS. Data entered on one MCDU automatically transfers to the others. (Scott E. Germain)

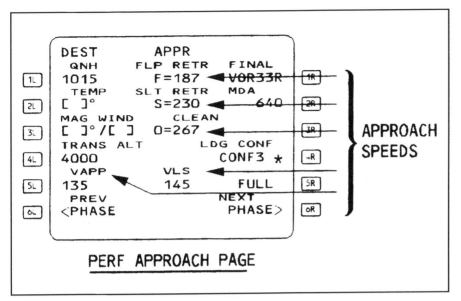

The MCDU PERF page contains aircraft speed and landing data for the approach to be flown. The left and right columns contain fields for the pilots to enter or modify data. (Airbus)

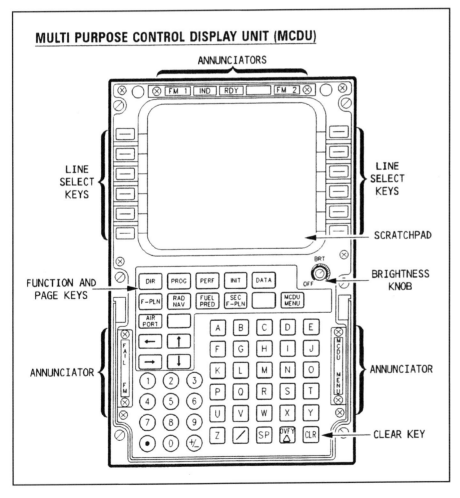

Each of the three MCDUs on the center pedestal have cross-talk ability; information entered on one is exported to the others. (Airbus)

navaids, routes, and waypoints stored by the pilot.

F-PLN calls up the Flight Plan A and B pages, a leg-by-leg display of the current flight plan waypoints. The slewing keys can be used to scroll up or down through the waypoints to make lateral or vertical revisions.

RAD NAV calls up the Radio Navigation page and displays the navaids auto-tuned by the FMGCs.

FUEL PRED calls up the Fuel Prediction page. Once the engines are started, this page displays the calculated fuel remaining at the destination and alternate airports, and other fuel management data.

SEC F-PLN calls up the secondary, or backup, flight plan. This is normally a copy of the primary flight plan, and is modifiable.

MCDU MENU displays the subsystems available through the MCDU. Accessing these subsystems is done by using the Line Select Key next to the name of the desired system.

AIRPORT calls up the flight plan page that includes the next airport along the current flight plan. The first push of the key displays the destination, and a successive push shows the alternate airport.

Once the flight plan and aircraft performance data is entered into the MCDU and verified, the FMGS has all of the necessary data to guide the aircraft along the programmed route of flight. Once airborne, the FMGS – through the autopilot – will acquire and track the Managed or Selected flight path; climb, cruise, and descend at preset speeds; and fly an instrument approach to an autolanding if necessary. If poor visibility results in a missed approach, the autopilot will also fly the missed approach procedure; all the flight crew must do is move the thrust levers to the MCT detent and reconfigure the aircraft. The autopilot also controls nosewheel steering to main-

tain the runway centerline after an autolanding.

The automation built into the A340 is complex, and a unique system had to be devised to enable the pilots to observe which autoflight modes are armed or active. The solution is called the Flight Mode Annunciator (FMA), and is built into the top of the Primary Flight Display (PFD). Five rows display the armed or engaged status of the Autothrust, lateral and vertical modes of the autopilot, the flight director, and approach capability. The multicolored alphanumeric display gives the pilot a quick-look ability to ensure the proper modes are armed or active.

Cockpit Displays

As with other modern jet transports, the A340 is equipped with an Electronic Flight Instrumentation System (EFIS). Two Primary Flight Display (PFD), two Navigation Display (ND), and two Electronic Centralized Aircraft Monitoring (ECAM) screens provide the pilots with full time flight guidance, navigation, and system advisory information throughout all phases of flight. EFIS control panels are located at each end of the glareshield and are used to control their respective PFD and ND screens.

The PFDs combine several flight instruments into one color display. The flight director, instrument approach guidance, altitude, heading, and airspeed information are displayed, as well as normal pitch and bank data. The NDs have arc (map), compass rose (NAV), Compass Rose VOR, Compass Rose ILS and Plan modes. The normal arc mode shows the aircraft at the bottom center with the course line ahead and toward the top. Waypoints, descent points, level off points, and referenced crossing restrictions are also displayed in color. A heading band is displayed along the top edge.

Two ECAM screens occupy the

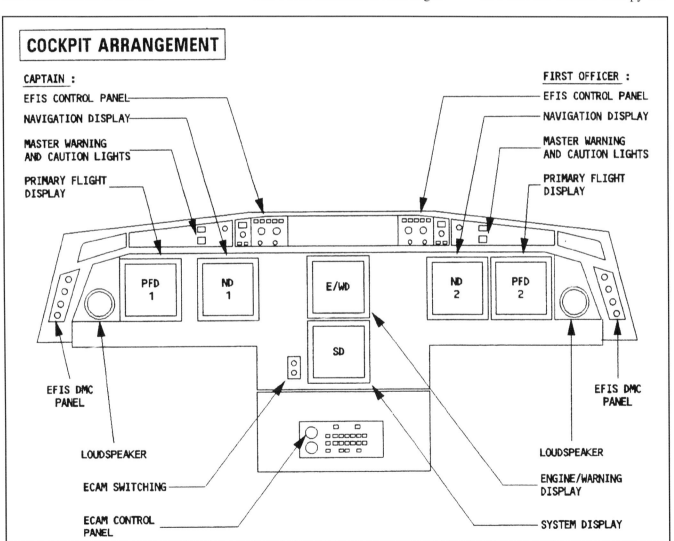

Layout of the cockpit instrument panel. (Airbus)

EFIS PRIMARY FLIGHT DISPLAY (PFD)

The Flight Management generates the following information :
- Armed and engaged modes on the Flight Mode Annunciator (FMA)
- FMGS guidance targets (SPD, ALT, HDG)
- Vertical deviation from descent profile
- Messages
- Navigation information

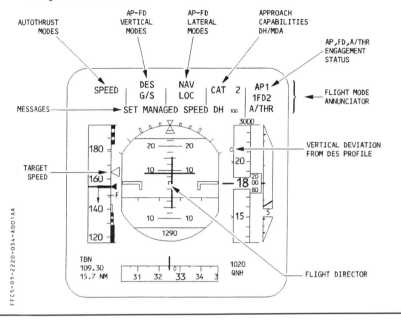

EFIS NAVIGATION DISPLAY (ND)

Flight Management (FM) generates the following information :
- aircraft position
- flight plans (active, secondary, temporary, and dashed)
- lateral deviation from primary flight plan
- pseudo waypoints along the flight plan
- raw data from tuned navaids
- wind information
- various options, depending on what the pilot selects on the EFIS control panel : waypoints, navaids, NDBs, airports, constraints
- type of approach selected
- messages

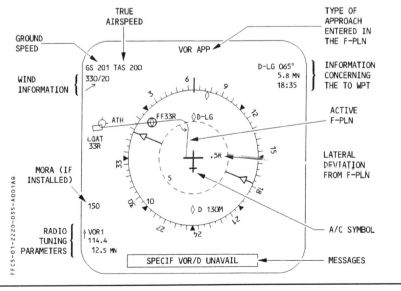

Layout of the Primary Flight Display (PFD). The upper portion, called the Flight Mode Annunciator (FMA), informs the pilots of the armed or captured status of the autopilot, autothrust, and approach modes. All symbology is color coded. (Airbus)

center instrument panel. The upper screen serves as the Engine/Warning Display (E/WD), and is divided into three sections. The main section contains graphical engine symbology for N1, EGT, N2, and fuel flow. Fuel on board and the flaps/slats position is also displayed. The memo section, on the lower left portion of the screen, alerts the crew to the temporary operation of certain systems, and displays the takeoff or landing memo at the proper time. The lower right portion of the screen contains the warning/caution display, listing any failures and corresponding procedures to be performed.

Under the E/WD is the System Display (SD). Programmed logic in the screen switching software allows this screen to automatically switch when the phase of flight changes, or when the crew selects a page on the ECAM control panel. If a system failure occurs, the crew is notified via an aural and visual warning, and the corresponding screen is displayed with a title describing the failure, and a checklist to rectify the situation or secure the system. Operational status is then displayed to inform the crew of inoperative systems and flight limitations. Some information is always displayed on the bottom of the SD:

Shown in the NAV mode, the Navigation Display (ND) also has color-coded symbology to display various types of information to the flight crew. Weather radar data is automatically scaled and displayed ahead of the aircraft's position. (Airbus)

Total Air Temperature, Static Air Temperature, Universal Coordinated Time, Gross Weight, and current Center of Gravity.

Any system page can be called up by the pilot on the ground or in flight. These include ENGINE, BLEED, CAB PRESS, ELEC AC, ELEC DC, HYD, C/B, APU, COND, DOOR/OXY, WHEEL, F/CTL, FUEL, and CRUISE pages. The system screens that appear on the lower ECAM use colored graphical diagrams that show the related system. In general terms, a simple schematic of the system is displayed that shows the status of valves, pumps, generators, or any other component. In a quick glance, the pilot can see that everything is normal, or what part of the system has been affected by a failure. Normal system operations are displayed in green, while portions of a system that have failed or that shut down are displayed in amber.

In normal cruise flight, the CRUISE page is on the lower ECAM screen. Fuel used, oil quantity, and N1/N2 vibrations levels of each engine are shown. On the bottom of the screen, the temperature of the cockpit and forward, mid, and aft cabins are shown. Cabin differential psi, altitude, and rate of climb/descent are also displayed.

The ECAM control panel is also equipped with a T.O. CONFIG push button, allowing the crew to test the aircraft configuration before takeoff. The test insures the cabin signs are on, the cabin is ready for takeoff, the spoilers are armed, the flaps are in the takeoff setting, and the autobrakes are set to MAX. If any item has not been set correctly, it remains blue on the Takeoff Memo and triggers a warning chime when the T.O. CONFIG button is pressed.

Electrical System

While parked at the gate, the A340 electrical system can be powered by dual ground-power receptacles near the nose gear of the aircraft. The APU can also provide power, or be used in concert with ground power. Two 37 amp-hour batteries are permanently connected to two hot busses, but only power a small portion of the electrical system. A dedicated battery to start the APU is located near the tail.

In flight, the 115/200 volt 400-hertz constant-frequency AC and 28-volt DC systems are supplied by four engine-driven AC generators, each supplying up to 75 KVA. Two generators are required to supply the entire system with power. Protection of electrical components is provided by circuit breakers located in the below-deck electronic equipment bay. A Circuit Breaker Monitoring Unit (CBMU) keeps tabs on each circuit breaker and displays relay this information to the ECAM system.

The A340 electrical system was designed to continue operating even with multiple failures. The APU,

Getting a heavy A340 stopped creates a tremendous amount of heat within the brakes, so cooling fans have been incorporated into the wheels. The lower ECAM can display the WHEEL page to show the temperature of each brake. The setting sun catches TAP Air Portugal's CS-TOA after landing at Frankfurt. TAP utilizes the aircraft in its intended role of an L-1011, and even an A310, replacement aircraft. (Ulrich Hoppe)

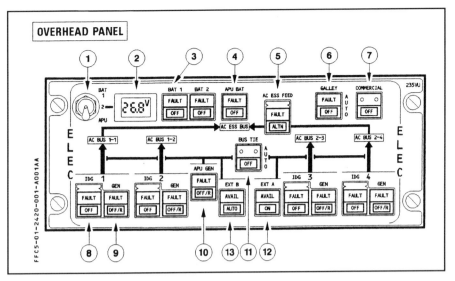

The ELEC portion of the overhead panel contains all controls for the system. The guarded IDG push button mechanically disconnects the generators from the engine gearbox. (Airbus)

Ram Air Turbine (RAT), aircraft batteries, and a generator driven by green hydraulic system pressure can all supply electrical power, albeit in a reduced capacity. Automatic load shedding will occur, with the flight crew being notified via the System Display.

The Cockpit

The basic A340 cockpit design is almost an exact copy of the Airbus A320, which allows transitioning flight crews to become comfortable in a very short period of time. Between the A320, A330, and A340, all controls, displays, and switches are placed in the same locations, with small changes to suit the specific aircraft. The system automation and cockpit design philosophy requires only two pilots to fly the A340, with no need for a flight engineer.

As with the A320, Airbus continued the "Lights Out" philosophy in the A340 cockpit. This philosophy centers on the premise that under normal conditions, the cockpit is dark, and no indication lights are visible. This is possible because each system push button on the overhead panel was designed with a white status light, and an amber failure light. To properly configure the systems, the crew simply pushes in all of the push buttons with white lights.

If a failure should occur, the affected component's push button will illuminate with an amber FAULT indication. The FAULT light and a chime draws the crew's attention to that item, and a checklist is automatically displayed on the lower

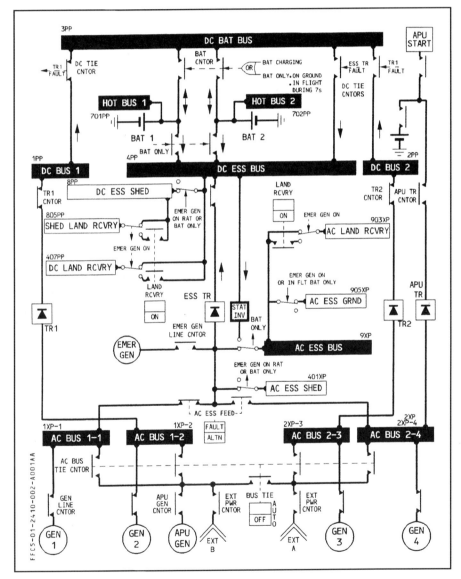

Simplified schematic of the A340 AC and DC electrical system. Power sources are arranged along the bottom of the diagram. (Airbus)

ECAM. The checklist will either rectify the problem, or secure the system if the fault cannot be reset.

All cockpit indications follow a color-coded architecture. Red indications signal a failure or situation that requires immediate crew action. Amber lights draw attention to failures that require flight crew awareness but no immediate action. Green indications inform the crew external or APU power is available. Blue lights indicate the normal operation of a temporary system. White lights draw attention to the abnormal position of a system push button. Push buttons on the system panel are pressed in for ON, AUTO, or OVRD, and out or released for OFF or MAN.

Both pilot seats are installed on tracks and allow electric or manual adjustments fore, aft, and vertically. Recline and lumbar adjustments are also available, and adjustable head-rests are also installed. Precise arm and hand placement for the side sticks is made easy by adjustable outboard arm rests, with markings for elevation and angle settings. The simple inboard armrests are adjustable in elevation only. All cockpit seats, including two jumpseats, are equipped with five-point quick-release harnesses.

Flight Controls

Generally speaking, the A340's Fly By Wire flight control system provides aircraft control, flight enve-lope definition/protection, and redundancy in case of hydraulic or computer failures. In general, the FBW system makes the A340 and similar Airbus' safer, more cost-effective, and more pleasant to fly.

Instead of using heavy mechanical means to actuate the flight controls, the basic FBW system uses wires and computer controlled electronic signals. The signals are routed to hydraulic actuators that move the desired control surface. The horizontal stabilizer and rudder have mechanical redundancy built in to prevent loss of control if multiple computer or hydraulic failures should occur.

Just like many other aircraft, the flight crew uses the sidesticks and rudder pedals to maneuver the air-

The A340 cockpit is a roomy work environment for the two-man flight crew. All controls and displays are within easy reach of both pilots, and provide quick monitoring and control of all systems. The center pedestal contains the two primary MCDUs, radios, thrust levers, engine master switches, speed brake lever, and the flap handle. A third MCDU and a full-sized printer are located near the bottom. (Scott E. Germain)

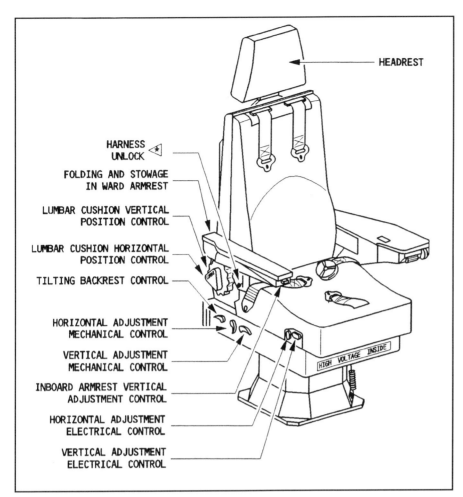

HEADREST

HARNESS UNLOCK

FOLDING AND STOWAGE IN WARD ARMREST

LUMBAR CUSHION VERTICAL POSITION CONTROL

LUMBAR CUSHION HORIZONTAL POSITION CONTROL

TILTING BACKREST CONTROL

HORIZONTAL ADJUSTMENT MECHANICAL CONTROL

VERTICAL ADJUSTMENT MECHANICAL CONTROL

INBOARD ARMREST VERTICAL ADJUSTMENT CONTROL

HORIZONTAL ADJUSTMENT ELECTRICAL CONTROL

VERTICAL ADJUSTMENT ELECTRICAL CONTROL

HIGH VOLTAGE INSIDE

The pilot seat of the A340 is fully adjustable with manual and electric controls. The outboard arm rests adjust to provide proper arm, wrist, and hand placement for the side stick controller. (Airbus)

craft. Flight Control computers receive signals from the sidesticks and rudder pedals and move the flight control surfaces to comply with the pilot's commands. However, the computers in the FBW system prevent loss of control during excessive maneuvering and prevent flight outside of the approved envelope.

Each pilot has a sidestick controller for manual control of pitch and roll. Yaw is automatically controlled by the logic in the flight control software. Five flight control computers are the heart of the A340 flight control system. They process pilot and autopilot inputs, and function in Normal, Alternate, or Direct flight control laws.

Three Flight Control Primary Computers (FCPC) control logic for normal, alternate, and direct flight control laws, speed brake and ground spoiler control, and compute the characteristic speeds displayed on the PFD speed tape.

Two Flight Control Secondary Computers (FCSC) manage the direct control law, yaw damping, rudder trim, rudder travel, and rudder pedal travel limits.

Two Flight Control Data Concentrator (FCDC) computers acquire data from the PRIM and SEC computers, and relay it to the EIS (Electronic Instruments System) and CMC (Central Maintenance Computer).

During normal operations one

master PRIM computer processes flight control signals either from the autopilot or the sidesticks, rudder pedals, spoiler lever, and thrust levers. These signals are sent to the other computers for execution and flight control movement. The secondary PRIM computers can also serve as the master. If one of the secondary computers is not able to execute the orders sent by the master, another computer executes the task of the affected computer except for spoiler control.

Each elevator is independently driven by a servojack for pitch control redundancy. Movement ranges from 30° up to 15° down. If flight control laws degrade due to multiple failures, the Trimmable Horizontal Stabilizer (THS) can move between 14° up and 2° down for pitch control. The THS is also controlled by two separate hydraulic actuators through a single screwjack.

Roll control on the A340 comes from inboard and outboard ailerons on each wing. Driven by pressure from each of the hydraulic systems, the ailerons can deflect up to 25° degrees for roll control, and droop for improved low-speed handling characteristics when the flaps are lowered. Above 190 KTS, the outboard ailerons are controlled to the zero deflection position, allowing the inboard ailerons to control roll. Certain flight control failure modes will allow the use of the outboard ailerons up to 300 KTS. Five of the six spoilers on each wing assist in roll control, and double as in-flight speed brakes. Controlled by a lever on the center pedestal, deflection can be modulated up to the 30° maximum.

All six spoiler surfaces are used as ground spoilers to dump lift after the aircraft touches down. When the spoiler lever is placed in the armed position, the spoilers automatically deploy when the main landing gear

touches down and the thrust levers are brought to idle. If a takeoff is rejected above 72 KTS, the spoilers will also deploy when the thrust levers are brought to idle.

Each wing has an inner and outer flap and seven slat surfaces for increasing lift at low speeds. A five-position FLAPS lever on the center cockpit pedestal electrically controls the hydraulically actuated surfaces. Two Slats Flaps Control Computers (SFCC), each having one flap and one slat channel, monitor and run the system, while a Power Control Unit (PCU) provides power via two separate hydraulic actuators. Blue and Green hydraulic pressure power the slats, while Green and Yellow hydraulic pressure power the flaps. When the slat or flap surfaces have reached the selected position, Pressure-Off Brakes (POB) lock the surfaces in place. The POB also performs the same function if a hydraulic power failure occurs.

Control Laws

Airbus designers used data generated by previous airline accidents and years of experience to build logic into the A340 flight control system. In simple terms, an A340 in normal operations will not allow the flight crew to exceed certain pitch, bank, and G parameters. If these limits are never exceeded, the aircraft will never be lost due to flight outside the approved envelope. Since

When selected to Flaps One or greater, the inner and outer ailerons droop 10° for improved low-speed handling. Without hydraulic pressure on the ground, they droop fully to 25°. The upturned winglets increase the efficiency of the A340 by decreasing drag-producing wingtip vortices. (Scott E. Germain)

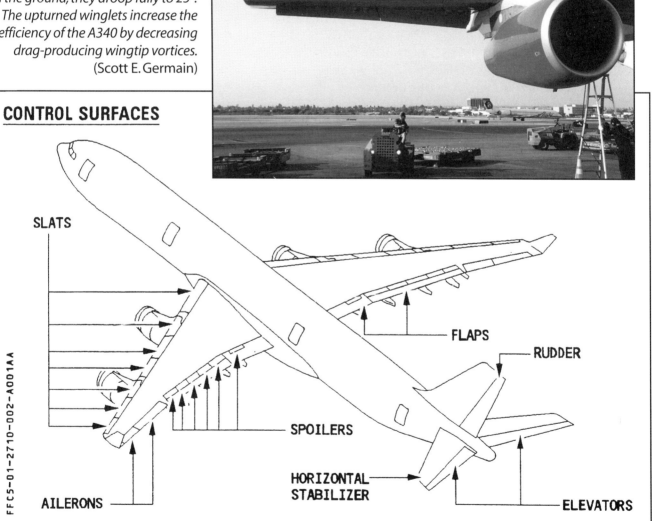

CONTROL SURFACES

SLATS

FLAPS

RUDDER

SPOILERS

HORIZONTAL STABILIZER

AILERONS

ELEVATORS

FFC5-01-2710-002-A001AA

Flight control surfaces of the A340. (Airbus)

excessive angle of attack and loss of airspeed have been causative factors in many commercial aircraft accidents, Airbus designed a system to prevent such a scenario.

Normal flight control law in the A340 provides control about all three flight axis, flight envelope protection, and maneuver load alleviation. Depending on the phase of flight, the flight control computers provide several different modes of pitch control. Switching between the different modes is transparent to the pilot, and occur automatically.

Because the takeoff is such a critical phase of flight, the A340 system gives the pilot full elevator authority in Direct Law. A direct relationship between sidestick position and elevator position exists for full, crisp control inputs while close to the ground. Once airborne and climbing, the Flight Mode automatically changes to a 1 G load factor schedule. While in flight, the aircraft will maintain the programmed 1 G unless stick inputs are made that require more G load, up to certain limits.

The control mode changes again when the aircraft is in the landing configuration and passes through 100 AGL. The FBW system reverts back to Direct Law, but retains some control damping through load-factor and pitch-rate feedback loops. This allows precise corrections to be made during the landing in gusty wind conditions.

Throughout the entire flight envelope, the flight control system automatically pitch trims for changes in airspeed, angle of attack, or configuration. This function works during manual flight, or with the autopilot engaged. When hand flying, the pilot simply sets a pitch attitude or rolls into a turn with the proper pitch and releases the stick. Only small corrections are required to maintain the desired setting.

Protections

In Normal Law, the flight control computers provide complete flight envelope protection concerning load factor, pitch attitude, high Angle of Attack (AOA), and high speed. In Airbus parlance, these are called "Prots" which is short for *protections*.

The A340's load factor Prot limits the aircraft to +2.5/-1 G with the slats up, and +2/-0 G with the slats extended. Pitch is limited to 30° nose up, with a progressive reduction to 25° nose up at lower airspeeds. The nose down limit is 15°. All pitch limits are displayed on the PFD scale as small green "=" symbols.

To prevent stalling, the flight control system incorporates an angle of attack Prot. Taking weight and configuration into account, the AOA limits are indirectly displayed on the PFD airspeed tape as colored vertical bars. They inform the flight crew a critical, low speed area is being entered.

"Alpha Prot" is displayed as the upper limit of an amber bar, and signifies the maximum steady-state AOA the aircraft can fly. The lower end of the amber and black portion of the band is "Alpha Max," a limit the pilot cannot fly past. If the aircraft were able to fly past Alpha Max, it would stall. Airbus opponents say

Welcome to America! A Lufthansa A340 touches down at Philadelphia after flying direct from Germany. The articulating main landing gear works to help trim the pitch attitude during takeoff and landing, preventing high pitch rates and tail scrapes. (Richard Chase)

that this is taking control away from the pilots, but it actually allows much more precise control of AOA and gives a better chance of recovery before contacting the terrain.

Somewhere between Alpha Prot and Alpha Max is "Alpha Floor," the point where the flight control system automatically activates the AOA Prot. When this occurs, the autothrust selects TOGA thrust, the autopilot kicks off, and the sidestick switches to direct control of AOA, not aircraft pitch. Even holding full aft stick will not allow the aircraft to exceed Alpha Max and enter a stall. If the pilot releases the stick, the AOA returns to Alpha Prot and remains there. Pushing the stick forward 8 degrees and lowering the AOA will end the protection and the system will return to Normal control law.

Overspeed protection is available through a nose-up pitch application when the airspeed passes V_{MO} + 6 KTS, or M_{MO} + 0.01 Mach. Even if the pilot pushes full nose down on the stick, it cannot overpower the Prot once it reaches V_{MO} + 15 KTS or M_{MO} + 0.04 Mach. If the stick is held full forward in this overspeed situation, the airspeed will stabilize between V_{MO} and V_{MO} + 15 KTS. Any overspeed condition will deactivate the autopilot and generate a continuous repetitive chime. The Prot deactivates when the overspeed condition ends.

Roll Prots in Normal Law prevent excessive bank angles and give positive spiral stability above 33° of bank. For all turns up to 33° of bank, the pilot simply rolls into the turn and centers the stick. The flight control system will automatically hold the bank angle until another stick input is made. If the angle of bank is greater than 33°, the pilot will have to hold that angle with stick input. If the stick is released, the aircraft will automatically

Air Lanka, currently undergoing a face lift to SriLankan, shows off the new livery in this photo. The airlines flies four A340s in addition to A320 and A330 aircraft. (Airbus)

reduce the bank angle to 33°. The maximum bank angle is 67° as marked by green "=" symbols on the PFD bank scale.

The logic in the flight control system also limits bank angle when other Prots activate. Upon reaching Alpha Floor, bank angle is limited to 45°, and high-speed Prot activation will reduce bank angle to zero without any pilot input. If a turn needs to be made, only 45° of bank will be available.

Just considering the Normal flight control law, the level of sophistication in the A340 flight control system is truly impressive. Even more impressive, however, are the failure modes built into the system architecture. These modes provide reduced levels of automation and protections, but prevent reversion to manual control or losing a system outright. The three levels of flight control reconfigurations are Alternate Law (two different modes), Direct Law, and Mechanical.

Alternate Law 1 is entered when failures occur in certain systems related to the flight control surfaces, PRIM ability, or a single Air Data Reference (ADR) unit. In this mode, pitch control reverts to Alternate Law while the lateral control remains in Normal Law. Only pitch attitude and low energy protections are lost.

More serious problems such as total engine failure, double ADR or IR faults, all spoilers faulting, or inboard aileron faults will deride the flight control system to Alternate Law 2. In this case, pitch, low energy, and bank angle protections are lost. Lateral flight controls revert to Direct Law, where the aircraft is flown like any conventional aircraft. Yaw control reverts to Alternate law. The most serious failures would degrade the system to the Direct Law. Although the aircraft feels more sensitive and the protections are lost, the aircraft remains flyable with relatively good flight characteristics.

Even though this very simplified description seems complicated, the failure modes of the A340 allow the aircraft to continue flying with a higher degree of safety than other aircraft without FBW controls. If a generic transport jet were to suffer a major failure of a hydraulic system or a major flight control surface, a crash or serious accident may be the result. But in the Airbus world, these failures simply degrade the protections and allow the flight to continue and land safely.

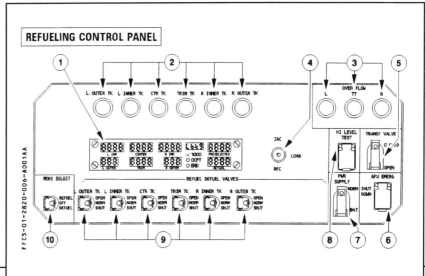

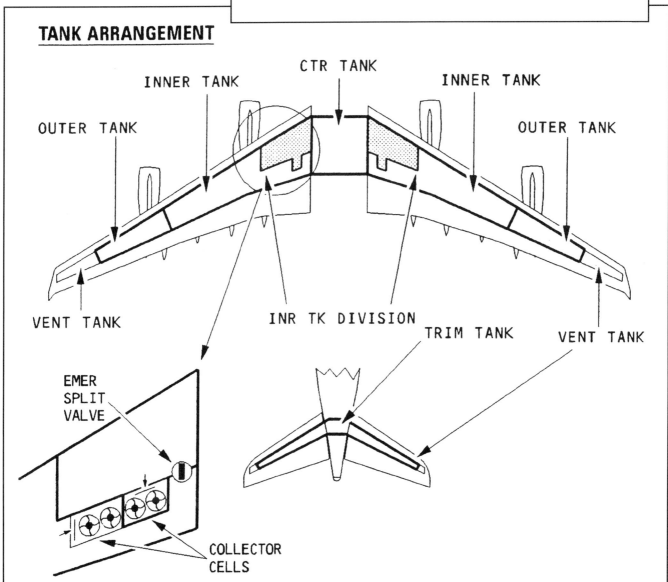

The A340 can tote 244,896 lbs. of fuel for long-range operations. Tank arrangement is shown (in main diagram) with associated collector cells. The Refueling panel diagram is shown in the inset. (Airbus)

Fuel System

Like many A340 systems, the fuel system is automated and requires little attention from the pilots. In addition to providing fuel to the engines and APU, the system provides fuel to cool the Integrated Drive Generators (IDGs) and to serve as ballast in the outer wing tanks. Fuel can also be transferred to the horizontal stabilizer to maintain an optimum center of gravity over the duration of a flight.

The tremendous amount of fuel for long-range flights is divided between wing tanks and a center fuselage tank. Each wing tank is divided into an inner and outer cell, holding 73,024 lbs. and 6,387 lbs. of fuel respectively. The outer tanks are connected to the inner tanks by transfer valves, which automatically open to transfer fuel to the inner tanks. A center tank capable of holding 72,205 lbs. of fuel is also fitted. The trim fuel tank built in to the horizontal stabilizer is normally not filled on the ground, but can hold up to 10,593 lbs. of fuel for in-flight CG control.

Expansion room for fuel is provided by surge tanks outboard of the wing tanks. These tanks have enough capacity to prevent fuel spillage, even if fuel temperatures rise by 20% C. The right portion of the trim fuel tank also has a surge tank. Overpressure protectors are built into each wing surge tank, the trim fuel surge tank, and in between the center and right inner tanks.

Fuel use and sequencing is automatically controlled by the Fuel Control and Monitoring System (FCMS). Between flights, the only crew actions necessary are defining the required fuel load before fueling and inserting the zero fuel weight and center of gravity position into the FMGS. Dual Fuel Control and Monitoring Computers (FCMC) pro-vide control of fuel transfer, refueling, quantity measuring and indication, level sensing, fuel temperature indication, and IDG fuel cooling control. The computers also provide aircraft gross weight and center of gravity calculations based on Zero Fuel Weight and Zero Fuel Center of Gravity as entered by the flight crew.

Fuel tank selection follows a complex schedule to preserve the aircraft's CG and lessen structural bending loads. As fuel can only feed from the inner tanks, the system is designed to transfer fuel to the inner tanks at preset levels.

When a flight begins, fuel is burned from the inner tanks to allow room for center tank fuel to continuously replace it. Once the center tank fuel has been complete-ly transferred to the inner tanks, the center pumps shut off, and the inner tanks burn down to approximately 11,000 lbs. When this level is reached, any fuel in the trim tank is pumped to the inner tank. Once again, the inner tanks are allowed to burn down to approximately 8,800 lbs., allowing the outer tank fuel to be transferred. The system normally runs automatically, but manual control is also available.

Due to the complexity of fail-ures and possible tank damage sce-narios, a high level of redundancy is built into the A340 fuel system. An X-FEED (crossfeed) valve is associated with each engine, and connects the engine and its associated pumps to the crossfeed line. This allows any pump to supply any engine on the aircraft. When fuel jettison is selected or if the aircraft enters the Emergency Electrical configuration, all X-FEED valves automatically open.

One of the design points of the A340 was the use of fuel to aid in pitch trim and CG optimization. Controlling the CG and positioning it precisely cuts drag dramatically, and allows the aircraft to fly more efficiently. The Trim Tank Transfer System handles these chores by shifting fuel between the trim tank located in the horizontal tail and the center or inner fuel tanks. Automatic fore or aft transfers are possible, as well as manual forward transfers.

Aft fuel transfer procedures automatically begin as the aircraft climbs through 25,500 MSL, and terminates when descending through 24,500 feet MSL. Logic built into the FMGC also shuts off the transfer when the calculated time to the des-tination is below one hour and fif-teen minutes. The trim tank is isolat-ed when the landing gear is extend-ed. Normally, only one aft fuel trans-fer is made during a flight.

Refueling the A340 can be accomplished from pressure refuel-ing couplings under each main wing. A refueling panel is located on the right fuselage side and beneath the right wing, while an optional refuel-ing panel can also be installed under the left wing. The refueling process allows a single fueler to select the required load on the refueling panel. A fuel gallery automatically fills each tank simultaneously with the required load.

When the desired fuel level in any tank is reached, that tank's refu-eling valve automatically closes. Total time to top off all fuel tanks with both wing pressure fueling ports being used is 33 minutes. Man-ual fueling is also available through over-wing ports. Pumps are then able to transfer fuel to the center tank or trim tank as necessary.

The A340 is also equipped with a 2,200 lb./min fuel jettison system. The system is manually activated through two JETTISON push but-tons on the overhead fuel control panel. Both push buttons must be pressed to begin the operation. When this is selected, all crossfeed

Each hydraulic system is controlled via the overhead panel. The RAT MAN ON guarded push button, when depressed, drops the Ram Air Turbine from the wing to provide green system pressure. (Airbus)

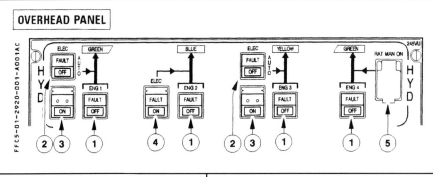

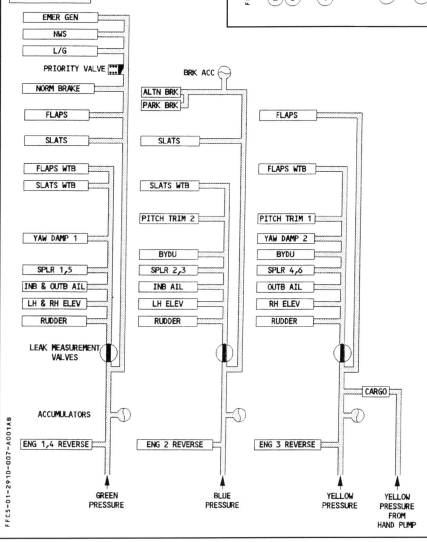

Distribution of Green, Yellow, and Blue hydraulic systems. (Airbus)

valves open and all main and stand-by fuel pumps operate. The jettison continues until the crew stops it, or when a preset quantity is reached.

Hydraulics

Three separate hydraulic systems equip the A340, and provide redundancy in case of hydraulic pump, engine, component, or flight control failure. Each 3,000 psi system provides pressure to different flight controls, high-lift devices, spoilers, and services. A Hydraulic System Monitoring Unit (HSMU) keeps tabs on each system and provides ECAM display data.

The green system is pressurized by pumps on engines one and four, and supplies pressure to the primary flight controls, landing gear, brakes, and yaw damper number one. An electric pump will automatically run if engines one and four are shut down, and further backup is provided by a Ram Air Turbine (RAT). Located in the right wing, the RAT can drop into the airflow, allowing a small propeller to spin. This action drives a hydraulic pump in the green circuit. Automatic RAT extension occurs if all four engines fail, if there is an electrical power loss when engines one and four are shut down, or if low fluid levels are detected in the Green or Blue reservoirs. The RAT may also be manually extended with the RAT MAN ON push button on the overhead panel.

Secondary hydraulics are provided by the yellow system. An engine-driven pump on number three engine and an automatic electrical pump ensure the system is always pressurized. Certain primary flight controls are powered by this system as backups, along with the flaps, yaw damping, trim, certain spoilers, and the cargo doors.

If a worst-case in-flight scenario should develop, the blue hydraulic system supplies hydraulic pressure to the inboard ailerons, the left elevator, rudder, slats, and alternate brakes as a means of getting the aircraft back on the ground. This sys-

tem is powered by a pump on the number two engine or a manual electric pump.

Landing Gear

The landing gear on the Airbus A340 consists of two inward-retracting main landing gear assemblies, a forward retracting center gear, and a forward retracting nose gear. Each are fully enclosed by electrically-controlled, hydraulically-actuated gear doors. During landing gear transit, all gear doors sequence open before and close after gear movement. The doors that attach to the landing gear struts operate mechanically via the movement of the landing gear legs.

Two Landing Gear Control and

The main and center landing gear of the A340 spread the weight of the aircraft over a wide area on the tarmac. The center landing gear retracts forward, while the main bogies compress six inches and retract inward. Gear doors always cycle shut after the landing gear moves. (Scott E. Germain)

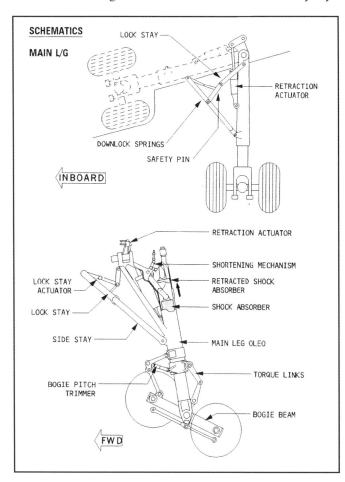

Main landing gear diagram showing extended and retracted positions and actuators. (Airbus)

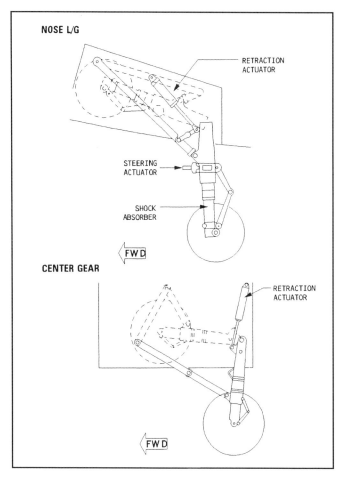

Nose and Center landing gear legs, actuators, and components. (Airbus)

Interface Units (LGCIU) process gear and gear door positions, system sequencing, and gear lever selection position. ECAM landing gear locked/unlocked indications and squat switch functions also originate from the LGCIUs.

Manufactured by Dowty, each main landing gear is a four-wheel, twin-tandem bogie with an oleo-pneumatic shock absorber. The shock absorber system is also fitted with a mechanism to retract the strut several inches, making the landing gear more compact during stowage. A hydraulically operated pitch trimmer is built into each gear bogie to dampen the movement and ensure the unit returns to its normal position after liftoff. Anti-skid brakes are fitted to each main landing gear assembly.

A center landing gear unit helps distribute the weight of the aircraft while on the tarmac. Attached to the rear bulkhead of the main landing gear bay, the center wheels are identical to the nose wheels for parts commonality. An oleo-pneumatic shock absorber is installed on this leg. The unit can also be locked in the retracted position by maintenance crews. In this case, the doors for the center landing gear will continue to operate during the retraction and extension sequence.

The nose landing gear, manufactured by Messier-Bugatti, features oleo-pneumatic shock absorption and a nosewheel steering actuator. Powered by the green hydraulic system, the steering is controlled by FBW tillers on each side of the cockpit, the rudder pedals, or signals from the autopilot. Up to 65° of nosewheel steering is available from the steering tillers, and by breaking a physical stop on the tiller, a maximum of 78° can be attained. An internal cam mechanism automatically returns the nosewheel to the centered position after takeoff.

In case of normal extension system failure, the A340 landing gear can be extended by gravity. This electromechanical system is controlled by two selectors located on the center instrument panel. When these are set to the down position, the hydraulic circuit of the landing gear is isolated, the gear doors unlock, and the gear extends by gravity. Springs assist in locking the gear down, however, the main landing gear doors will

The main landing gear wheels and tires of the A340 must soak up a tremendous load during landing, and the resultant heat from braking. The carbon brakes actually take time to heat up after the brakes are used, but electric cooling fans dissipate it quickly. The doors covering the main gear legs are made of carbon fiber. (Scott E. Germain)

remain open. The center landing gear remains retracted, and is not affected during this procedure.

Multi-disc, carbon brakes equip each main landing gear wheel and are actuated by either of two independent brake systems. Normally, green system hydraulic pressure is used, while the blue system and accumulator pressure are used as a backup. Braking commands originate from the brake pedals or the autobrake system. The Brake Steering Control Unit (BSCU) interprets these signals and applies normal or alternate brakes, autobrakes if selected, and antiskid control. The BSCU also performs secondary functions such as checking brake residual pressure, provides wheel speed data to other aircraft systems, and displays brake temperatures on the lower ECAM.

In the event of a wheel overheat, the main wheels are equipped with fusible plugs to vent tire pressure and prevent an explosion. At a certain temperature, the plugs melt and deflate the tire. Brake fans are installed to cool the brakes after heavy use or landings at high weights.

Navigation

The heart of the A340 lies in three separate Air Data and Inertial Reference Systems (ADIRS). The ADIRS take data from internal laser gyroscopes, accelerometers, pitot probes, static vanes, AOA probes, temperature probes, and navigation radios to derive current position, altitude, airspeed, and groundspeed. The gyros also provide attitude, heading, and bank angle information for the PFD.

The ADIRS is a smart system, but in order for it to do its job, it needs to know where it is. "Initializing" the IRS before each flight zeroes the system and allows a new

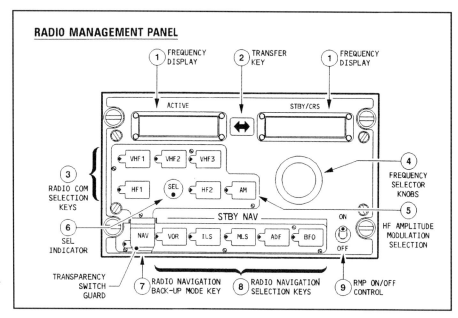

A source of consternation for new Airbus pilots; the Radio Management Panel (RMP). This unit controls the tuning of all onboard radios, and provides backup navigation tuning. (Airbus)

location to be entered, usually by punching in the city pair of the flight into the MCDU. Fine-tuning of position occurs when the thrust levers are brought up to the takeoff setting; the FMGS knows the exact lat/long of the runway used for takeoff, and updates position right there.

Once airborne, the FMGC will auto-tune the navigation radios along the route of flight. Global Positioning System (GPS) signals, VOR, ADF, DME, and ILS signals all provide data to the system for a high degree of navigation accuracy. Each FMGC tunes its on-side navigation receiver, but if one should fail, the other will control both receivers after activation of the Flight Management (FM) selector switch.

Manual tuning can also be used through the MCDU to override the FMGC's automatic selection and tuning of navaids. This does not affect the automatic function of the FMGC or the accuracy of navigation for the aircraft. If both FMGCs fail, the pilots can use their respective Radio Management Panel (RMP) to

manually tune VOR, ADF, and ILS stations. The captain's RMP controls VOR 1 and ADF 1, while the first officer's RMP controls VOR 2 and ADF 2. Each RMP can control either ILS 1 or 2.

Pneumatics

High-pressure air is supplied for cabin pressurization and air conditioning, engine starting, wing anti-ice, water tank pressurization, hydraulic reservoir pressurization, cargo bay heating, and pack bay ventilation. This "bleed air" is supplied from the engines, the APU, or two High Pressure (HP) ground connections.

Engine bleed air is automatically tapped from either the intermediate pressure stage or the high pressure stage, depending on the phase of flight. This hot, compressed air is routed through a precooler before entering the duct for use by the downstream pneumatic services. When the crossbleed switch is opened, a valve allows bleed air from any engine to enter the supply duct.

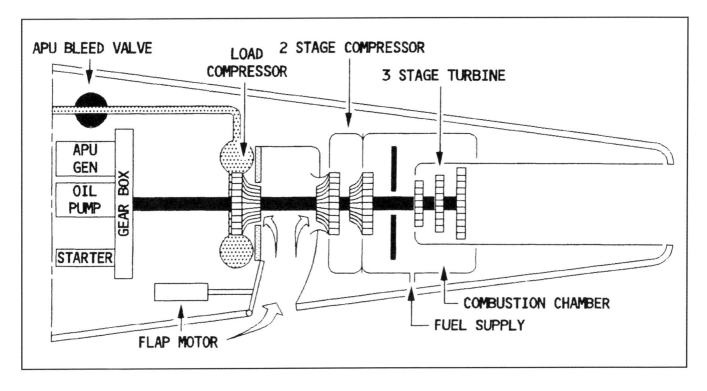

Diagram of the Allied-Signal APU, located in the tail of the A340. (Airbus)

APU bleed air can be used on the ground or in flight, and is controlled by the APU BLEED push button on the overhead control panel. When selected on, the APU provides bleed air to the system as long as the APU speed is over 95% RPM. This causes the APU bleed valve to open and the engine bleed valves to automatically close.

Auxiliary Power Unit

Mounted in the tail of the A340, the Auxiliary Power Unit (APU) is a small gas turbine engine that provides electric and pneumatic sources for various aircraft systems. Manufactured by Allied-Signal, the single-shaft engine provides bleed air from a load compressor, and electrical power from a generator.

Starting and operating the APU is fully automatic via the MASTER and START push buttons in the cockpit. The ECAM APU screen automatically displays when the START button is pressed, showing the start sequence and vital signs as the unit spools up. Once operating, the aircraft can be free of any external support equipment. During ground operations, the APU supplies bleed air for cabin air-conditioning and engine starting, as well as electrical power to run the aircraft's system.

Allied-Signal builds the GTCP 331-350C Auxiliary Power Unit. The rectangular air intake flap only opens when the APU is started and running, otherwise it closes to cut drag. The exhaust is ducted straight back through the tail cone. The small hole near the trailing edge of the left elevator is the APU oil cooler exhaust. (Scott E. Germain)

The APU's bleed air can be used in lieu of the engine's bleed supply to limit the reduction of available thrust during takeoff. With more thrust, the A340 is able to lift more weight on hot days at high altitude airports. APU bleed air may also be used in flight for cabin pressurization and air-conditioning, and the electrical generator can also provide an automatic back up to the four engine mounted generators.

Several safety measures allow the APU to be run without any crew supervision once the aircraft is parked. Automatic fire protection is provided by an auto-shutdown feature; if the APU fire loop senses heat over a certain limit, the APU will automatically shut down and dis-charge its fire-bottle. A horn sounds in the nose of the aircraft to notify the ground personnel. In the cockpit, an APU FIRE push button performs the same functions. Ground personnel can also shut down the APU by using the APU SHUT OFF push button on the interphone panel under the nose, or the APU EMER SHUT-DOWN push button on the refueling/defueling panel.

Doors

Three plug type passenger doors are located on each side of the fuselage for normal loading and unloading. Interior or exterior operation of these doors is assisted by hydraulic arms, allowing them to open out and forward easily. Operating the doors while armed will trigger the assist arms to automatically open the door and inflate the escape slides. Secondary handles allow crew members or passengers to manually inflate the slides if the automatic system fails.

Two emergency exit doors are located mid cabin, and allow additional escape paths from the aircraft. When opened, slides automatically inflate from a compartment below the door. Two sliding cockpit windows can also be used as emergency exits; each being equipped with an escape rope.

Two large cargo doors, one forward and one aft, open outward and up courtesy of yellow hydraulic system pressure. If yellow system pres-

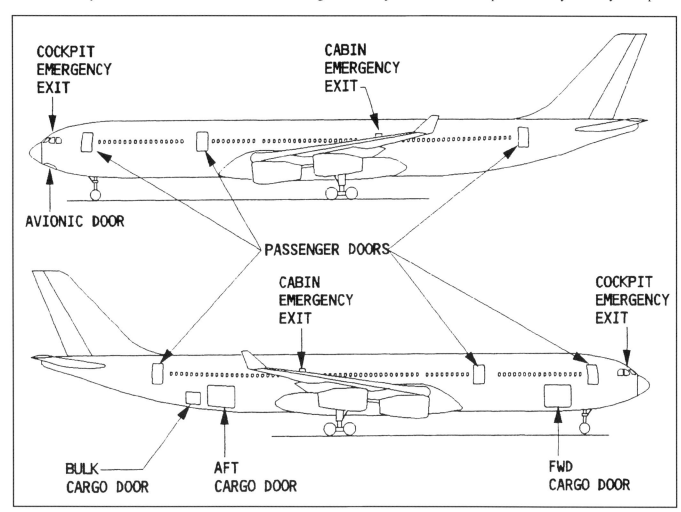

Location of each door on the A340-300. (Airbus)

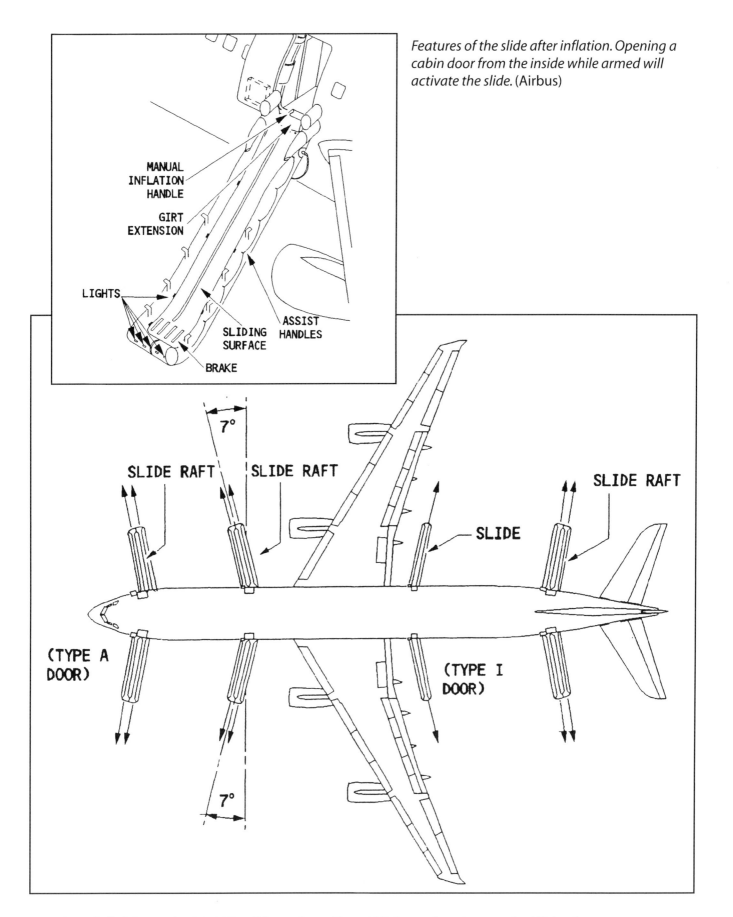

Features of the slide after inflation. Opening a cabin door from the inside while armed will activate the slide. (Airbus)

MANUAL INFLATION HANDLE

GIRT EXTENSION

LIGHTS

SLIDING SURFACE

ASSIST HANDLES

BRAKE

7°

SLIDE RAFT   SLIDE RAFT

SLIDE RAFT

SLIDE

(TYPE A DOOR)

(TYPE I DOOR)

7°

Location of all slides on the A340. The slides at doors 3L and 3R do not function as rafts. (Airbus)

sure is not available, hand pumps can be used to operate the doors. Mechanical locks ensure the doors are either locked open or closed. The rear bulk cargo door opens into the aft cargo area, and operates manually. All doors on the A340 are monitored by the Door and Slide Control System (DSCS), which generates all ECAM warnings and displays, as well as warnings on the doors themselves.

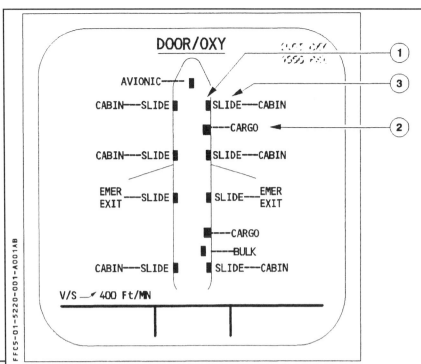

The ECAM Door/Oxy page shows the status of each door built in to the A340 fuselage. (Airbus)

The rear cargo and bulk cargo doors shown in the open position. Yellow hydraulic system pressure operates the cargo door, while the smaller bulk door is manually opened and locked up inside the fuselage. Lights are provided for night loading. (Scott E. Germain)

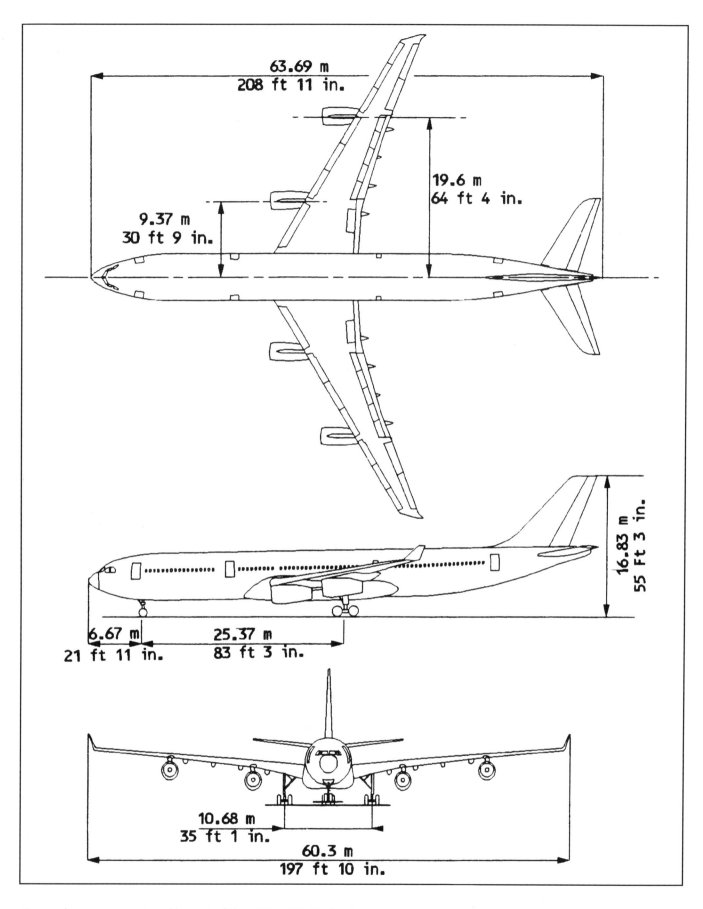

General arrangement and layout of the A340-300. (Airbus)

THE A340 IN COLOR

In modern airliners, most systems are divided into left or right, primary or secondary, AC or DC. It is somewhat fitting that the most modern of airliners, the Airbus A340, keeps up an Airbus tradition of color coding almost everything on the aircraft. Each hydraulic system is identified by a color; green, yellow, or blue.

More importantly, the symbology on the EFIS displays and MCDU windows in the cockpit are a mix of several colors, each giving a specific meaning to the flight crew. Indeed, the Airbus A340 is an aircraft of color, and the airlines that operate the four-engined, long-range aircraft keep the tradition with a bright selection of liveries.

Most airlines use simple stripes, stately fonts, and subdued colors to adorn their aircraft. With time ticking away on the millennium, airlines are now choosing more lavish color schemes to create excitement and a modern image. The following pages display not only the graceful lines of the A340, but the colorful and creative ways color is built into — and painted on — the aircraft.

Belgian airline Sabena displays a modern livery, and family commonality, during a formation photo shoot. The lead aircraft is a A330-300 with a A340-300 flying wing. Using the same fuselage and wing, the number of engines plays a large roll in how the aircraft is used in different markets. Long stage lengths make the 340 more attractive, while medium-length flights allow the A330 to generate more revenue.
(Airbus)

Registered as A7-HHK, the State of Qatar operates this sole A340-200 as a VIP transport. The Amiri Flight took delivery of the aircraft in May of 1993 and is equipped with a luxurious interior. (Ulrich Hoppe)

The exceptionally clean lines of the A340 can be appreciated in this photo. From an aerodynamicist's point of view, the aircraft is a very clean design, and allows a good combination of speed and efficiency with relatively low-thrust engines. (Airbus)

Singapore Airlines uses the range capabilities of the A340 to reach destinations far from the Asia base. A340-300E 9V-SJA, dubbed "CELESTAR" is shown after receiving its livery in the Airbus paint facility. Singapore Airlines operates 15 A340s, and has two more on order. (Airbus)

Although painted in Royal Brunei livery, the A340-200 is actually one of three owned by the Sultan of Brunei. Two are painted in this scheme, possibly as a means of keeping anonymity, and are used as personal aircraft. (Warbird Aero Services Collection)

More akin to a spaceship than an airliner, the flight deck of the A340 features the most advanced avionics in the industry. The interface between the crew and the FMGS is intuitive and functional. Tables extend from below the PFD/ND screens that can hold flight manuals, charts, or meal trays. Noise levels are extremely low due to improved air ducting within the ventilation system. (Airbus)

Airbus had listened to the airlines, and designed a well-lit, airy cabin. The lack of centerline overhead stowage leads to a feeling of open space, with ample coat closets and storage lockers for additional carry on items. (Airbus)

Iberia, Spain's flag carrier, operates eight A340-300 and has ordered 11 more examples. Only five seats are configured for first class, with 42 business class seats and 202 economy class seats. (Airbus)

System and equipment installation is done by Aerospatiale's St. Nazaire facility. Seen during transportation between the assembly area and the paint shop, much use is made of motorized assembly jigs such as this one. The three attachments on the fuselage side allow cranes to hoist the section during assembly. (Airbus)

Under 100 feet radar altitude, as measured to the main landing gear, the A340's autoflight system enters Direct Law for the landing. This provides more positive control close to the ground, while still providing a level of control damping. This Air Tahiti Nui A340-200 approaches the threshold at Los Angeles International Airport in February, 1999. Registered F-OITN, the aircraft displays one of the most colorful liveries ever put on an A340. (Mike Bednar)

OPERATING THE A340

Airbus officials use the term *commonality* a lot when they describe the relationship between their aircraft, especially the A330/A340. All Airbus designs have a similar look, and from the A320 onward, they even share a common cockpit and autoflight system. Design commonality even trickles down to small parts such as computers and Line Replaceable Units (LRUs), as many are common between the different aircraft. But the commonality Airbus really speaks of comes from a family of aircraft – from the A318 to the A340 – that have very similar flight and handling characteristics. The only real differences are getting used to the higher aircraft weight and the inertia it creates.

Getting the 375 passenger A340-300 to fly like the earlier A320 is possible with current FBW control systems. Although the layout of the flight control computers may be slightly different, the laws they use can be changed to modify the handling characteristics. Within reason, the ability exists to program certain flight characteristics with a desired "feel."

Since the aircraft have the same feel, commonality is further enhanced by using the same cockpit layout and flight displays. The cockpit layout and pilot viewpoint ease the transition from one aircraft to the other, allowing airlines to cross-utilize crews with minimum training costs. The most current information on flight crew/aircraft interface theories was used; the result being a state-of-the-art flight deck that is comfortable, roomy, and logical. Line-qualified Airbus pilots agree.

They all look and fly the same; from the A318 to the A340 pictured here. Commonality in flight characteristics is the heart of the Airbus family. (Airbus)

Flying the A340

A typical flight in the A340 begins with the first officer entering the flight deck and checking the status of the engine master switches, landing gear lever position, and powering up the aircraft electrical system. Engine oil and hydraulic fluid levels are checked on the respective ECAM pages, and a fire test is performed before starting the APU. Brake pressures are checked and the parking brake is set, flaps are checked up, and the air-conditioning is set to provide a comfortable cabin environment.

The exterior walk-around is similar to other turbine-powered aircraft and begins at the left forward fuselage. Continuing clockwise around the aircraft, typical items are checked for condition and wear. Particular attention must be paid to the pitot and static probes, AOA vanes, and oxygen bottle indicators; they are well above eye level and easy to miss.

Once the exterior inspection is complete, the flight crew performs specific duties as they ready the cockpit and the flight management system. Divided between captain and first officer, each system push button and switch is checked to ensure proper placement. One of the more important systems to check are the three ADIRUs, which require up to ten minutes for a full alignment.

Once the ADIRUs are aligning, the flight plan, weight data, and aircraft performance information can be entered into the FMGS. Since the database is customized for each airline, simply typing in the city pairs will enter the company-approved route into the flight plan. Modifications or changes are easily made, and a secondary flight plan can also be modified for enroute changes. Once the flight paperwork has arrived, actual Zero Fuel Weight and Block Fuel figures can be entered on the INIT B page, and takeoff speeds can be read from the appropriate speed card page.

Once the FMGS is programmed and the flying pilot briefs the takeoff, the captain will call for the before start checklist. After the cabin door is shut, pushback clearance is obtained and engine start can begin. The procedure calls for starting the number one and two engines ten seconds apart, which allows a seamless transfer of electrical power between the APU and the engine dri-

A more comfortable six-abreast Business Class layout is shown in the A340 mockup. Mixing first class and business class provides each traveler with a window or aisle seat and plenty of space to work. (Airbus)

Up to 33 LD3 cargo containers can be accommodated in the lower fuselage of the A340-300. Each container uses rollers for positioning in the pressurized and climate-controlled cargo hold. (Scott E. Germain)

The cargo doors are located on the right lower fuselage, and allow LD3 and outsized cargo to be loaded easily. Hydraulic pressure raises the door up where mechanical locks ensure the door doesn't fall. Dark outlines call attention to static and angle of attack sensors so ground crews won't damage them. (Scott E. Germain)

BEFORE START

COCKPIT PREP . . . . . COMPLETED (BOTH)	
GEAR PINS and COVERS . . . . REMOVED	
SIGNS . . . . ON / AUTO	
ADIRS . . . . NAV	
FUEL QUANTITY . . . . _____ KG.LB	
TO DATA / V. BUGS . . . _____ SET (BOTH)	
BARO REF . . . . SET (BOTH)	
WINDOWS/DOORS . . . . . CLOSED (BOTH)	
BEACON . . . . ON	
THR LEVERS . . . . IDLE	
PARKING BRAKE . . . . AS RQRD	

AFTER START

ANTI ICE . . . . AS RQRD	
ECAM STATUS . . . . CHECKED	
PITCH TRIM . . . . _____SET	
RUDDER TRIM . . . . ZERO	

BEFORE TAKEOFF

FLIGHT CONTROLS . . . . CHECKED (BOTH)	
FLT INST . . . . CHECKED (BOTH)	
BRIEFING . . . . CONFIRMED	
FLAP SETTING . . . . CONF – (BOTH)	
V1.VR.V2/FLX TEMP . . . . – (BOTH)	
ATC . . . . SET	
ECAM MEMO . . . . TO NO BLUE	
. SIGNS ON	
. SPLRS ARM	
. FLAPS TO	
. AUTO BRK MAX	
. TO CONFIG NORM	
CABIN CREW . . . . ADVISED	
ENG START SEL . . . . AS RQRD	
PACKS . . . . AS RQRD	

AFTER TAKEOFF / CLIMB

LDG GEAR . . . . UP	
FLAPS . . . . RETRACTED	
PACKS . . . . ON	
BARO REF . . . . SET (BOTH)	

APPROACH

BRIEFING . . . . CONFIRMED	
ECAM STATUS . . . . CHECKED	
V. BUGS . . . . _____ SET (BOTH)	
SEAT BELTS . . . . ON	
BARO . . . . _____ SET (BOTH)	
MDA/DH . . . . SET (BOTH)	
ENG START SEL . . . . AS RQRD	

LANDING

CABIN CREW . . . . ADVISED	
A/THR . . . . SPEED/OFF	
ECAM MEMO . . . . LDG NO BLUE	
. L/G DOWN	
. SIGNS ON	
. SPLRS ARM	
. FLAPS SET	

AFTER LANDING

FLAPS . . . . RETRACTED	
SPOILERS . . . . DISARMED	
APU . . . . START	
RADAR . . . . OFF/STBY	

PARKING

APU BLEED . . . . ON	
ENGINES . . . . OFF	
SEAT BELTS . . . . OFF	
EXT LT . . . . AS RQRD	
FUEL PUMPS . . . . OFF	
PARK BRK and CHOCKS. . . . . . .AS RQRD	

SECURING AIRCRAFT

ADIRS . . . . OFF	
OXYGEN . . . . OFF	
APU BLEED . . . . OFF	
EMER EXIT LT . . . . OFF	
NO SMOKING . . . . OFF	
APU . . . . OFF	
BAT 1+2+APU BAT . . . . OFF	

ON GROUND EMER / EVACUATION

– AIRCRAFT/PARKING BRK . . . . STOP/ON	
– ATC (VHF1) . . . . NOTIFY	
– ENG MASTERS (all) . . . . OFF	
– CABIN CREW (PA) . . . . NOTIFY	
– FIRE P/Bs (ENG and APU) . . . . PUSH	
– AGENTS (ENG and APU) . . . . AS RQRD	
– EVACUATION . . . . INITIATE	

CG	20	22	24	26	28	30	32	34	36	38
TRIM POS	UP	7		6	5	4	3	2	1	

FOCL-00-0007-001-A001AA

ARG ALL

The Normal Check List. (Airbus)

ven generators. When complete, engines three and four are started in the same manner. If a problem arises, the affected engines' FADEC will auto-abort and inform the crew via the lower ECAM.

Once all engines are running, slight breakaway thrust will get the A340 moving. Side mounted FBW steering tillers allow precise nose-wheel steering, and have little resistance to movement. Some care must be taken during turns, as the nose-wheel is located approximately 12 ft. behind the cockpit. Slight pressure on the toe-mounted FBW brakes provides smooth application with no tendency to grab. Flight crews transitioning to the A340 from smaller Airbus aircraft will soon understand overcoming the inertia of a 600,000 lb. aircraft will take considerably more distance than what they are used to.

The taxi check calls for testing the flight controls, configuring the flaps, setting autobrakes to MAX and configuring the engine bleed push buttons. Much of the time, lower takeoff weights allow A340 flight crews to perform reduced thrust, or "Flex," takeoffs. In this case, the thrust levers are placed in the FLX/MCT detent instead of TOGA. Flex takeoffs save engine wear, reduce fuel consumption, and lower noise levels.

Controlling the aircraft on the runway centerline is simple with the rudder pedals and nosewheel steering. As airspeed builds, the steering authority bleeds off and allows the rudder to maintain directional control.

Rotation forces in the A340 are artificially light, and only a slight pull on the sidestick is necessary to rotate. The Speed Reference System drives the flight directors for a 3°/sec. pitch rate to 12.5° nose up. Once the landing gear has been retracted and the aircraft climbs through 1,500 feet AGL and accelerates, the thrust levers

are placed in the CLMB detent until landing. Flaps are retracted as "F" and "S" speeds as displayed on the airspeed tape.

The A340 accelerates to 250 KTS rather quickly for such a large aircraft, and once passing 10,000 MSL, continues to accelerate to the climb speed entered on the MCDU CLMB PERF page. Hand flying the aircraft during the climb phase is a simple task and presents no special problems. Performance during the climb is impressive, generally taking less than six minutes from brake release to 10,000 feet. Pitch attitude during the climb depends on aircraft weight and airspeed, but in all cases visibility over the nose is excellent.

Hand flying the aircraft during climb brings a surprising characteristic to light – the FBW system provides control sensitivity more like that of a fighter or an aerobatic aircraft. Even though the stick has a surprisingly large range of movement, small inputs provide adequate responses without degrading maneuverability. Crisp inputs can be made for very precise pitch and roll control, even when flying in turbulence. Getting used to the sidestick generally takes a very short period of time, and requires little physical effort.

The autoflight system built into the A340 does an admirable job throughout the entire flight envelope. Most pitch, roll, and engine thrust inputs are smooth transitions with few abrupt changes. The system really shines when poor weather, complicated approach procedures, and a tired flight crew make use of the autopilot. Either of the two dual channel autopilots can be turned on at 100 feet AGL after takeoff and used throughout the flight. Use of both autopilots is required when using the autoland function.

Once at altitude, there is not much to do except monitor the progress of the flight, check the fuel burn, and ensure fuel is transferring properly. Performance figures generally show the A340 cruises 2° nose high at .84 Mach while burning 15,500 lbs./hr. The flight deck and cabin are extremely quiet, thanks to reworked baffling in the air supply ducts. A small amount of external wind noise is audible.

Airwork in the A340 is not particularly difficult. Decelerating for slow flight gives an opportunity to use the speed brakes, which are very effective. A lever on the center console activates spoilers one through six, with maximum deflection available up to the Flaps 2 setting. Full deployment quickly slows the A340 with a light airframe rumble.

In Normal Law with all flight control computers working, the aircraft can be maneuvered rather aggressively at low speed without fear of stalling. Even during rolling pitch ups, no buffeting occurred.

Further slow flight and stall

Flare and flash are calling cards of Richard Branson's Virgin Atlantic. With a flying blonde on each side of the nose, Virgin's A340s are slated to receive new paint liveries as this book goes to press. (Scott E. Germain)

demonstrations were flown, with several flight control computers selected off to degrade the flight control laws. Now in Alternate Law, the built-in AOA protection was lost, replaced by the natural stability of the aircraft. This condition is comparable to normal flight control modes of other transport category aircraft without FBW systems.

Throughout the maneuver, the A340 exhibited solid manners for a large aircraft. During one power-off stall, AOA reached approximately 25 units with the flaps at the 26° setting. Applying full power and lowering the nose allowed the aircraft to fly out of the stall and gain altitude quickly. Care must be taken not to use ailerons for roll control, as their use also activates the spoilers.

If further failures should occur, the A340 flight control system will again degrade to the Direct Law, a state comparable to flying another jet without the stability augmentation system engaged. Control of the aircraft is still relatively easy to maintain, but the controls become extremely sensitive. No protections are available in this configuration. All Airbus flight crews practice these scenarios in full motion flight simulators, and find it easy to recover from full stalls, unusual attitudes, and perform manual instrument approaches to a landing.

Steep turns can be flown very accurately by using the Flight Path Vector, a symbol on the PFD that shows where the aircraft is headed in space. One simply rolls into a 45° bank, and through the flight controls, holds the FPV on the horizon line. The airspeed trend arrow allows thrust to be modulated for airspeed control.

Descent planning in the A340 is a simple task, although the system is not foolproof. Based on waypoint crossing or speed restrictions, the FMGS will figure a descent point and display a white line with a downward arrow on the ND. This arrow informs the crew when it is time to go down, based on the descent speed entered on the DES PERF page. A typical descent profile of .83 Mach and 340 KTS can be modified by the crew. Deceleration to 250 KTS at 10,000 MSL is also automatic.

During the descent, a magenta doughnut appears on the PFD next to the vertical speed tape, and acts as a graphical display of where the aircraft is in relation to the descent profile. If the aircraft is above the profile, the doughnut will be near the bottom of the vertical speed tape. This prompts the pilot to increase the rate of descent to capture the profile. If the aircraft is below the profile, the doughnut appears near the top of the

One of the more lively paint schemes belongs to this Royal Brunei A340-200. The autoflight system uses dual radar altimeters and the autopilots for autoland capability. (P. Johnston)

Once the engines are brought into the CLB detent, and the slats and flaps are retracted, airspeed builds rapidly during the climb. From brake release, a typically loaded A340 will climb through 10,000 feet MSL in approximately six minutes.
(Karl Cornil)

The new Sabena paint scheme is displayed on OO-SCW. High AOA maneuvering in the A340 is a non-event due to the FBW system and its built-in protections. (Karl Cornil)

vertical speed tape. In either case, accessing the PROG page will display the actual number of feet the aircraft is above or below the profile.

Even though the A340 can fly a managed approach all the way to touchdown, hand-flying the aircraft presents no inherent problems. Vectors by air traffic control normally allow the flight to intercept the ILS localizer outside the outer marker. Use of the airspeed, heading, and altitude knobs on the FCU allow the flying pilot to quickly dial in new air traffic directions, leaving aircraft control to the autopilot.

Configuration changes are made with the Flap selector on the center pedestal, with five positions available. Only when Flap 2 is selected is there any noticeable change in attitude. When the flaps slide back and down, the nose of the A340 bumps down several degrees and requires attention while hand flying. Other flap settings have little or no effect on pitch.

For an ILS approach, the LOC push button on the FCU is selected to arm the localizer capture and tracking function. When the air traffic controller clears the flight for the approach, the APPR push button is used to arm both the localizer and glide slope capture modes. The aircraft will intercept the ILS and track it down to the runway. If necessary, the glide slope can also be captured from above.

Non-precision instrument approaches can also be flown, and are set up by using the Quick Reference Handbook (QRH). Short checklists in the QRH can be consulted to configure the autoflight system for the specific type of approach, whether it be a VOR, NDB, LOC, or RNAV. For most non-precision approaches, the FMGS will figure the proper descent profile and fly it much like an ILS. Flight crew workload during these approaches is greatly reduced.

A go-around from a missed approach is a simple matter in the Airbus. If decision height or minimum descent altitude is reached and the runway is not in sight, the flying pilot simply pushes the thrust levers to the TOGA detent and makes the necessary commands to reconfigure the aircraft. The FMGC will guide the aircraft along the published missed approach and enter the appropriate holding pattern automatically.

For this flight, the FMGS figured V_{APP} to be a very sedate 139 KTS at a landing weight of 402,000 lbs. Hand flying the aircraft on the ILS while following the flight director is simple; the A340's flight control system drastically reduces the workload. Hand flying raw data instrument approaches are also relatively easy; the flying pilot simply flies, and the non-flying pilot sets up the necessary flight director functions and configures the aircraft when called for. Visual approaches can make use of the autoflight and flight director capabilities, or the pilot can turn it all off and simply fly the aircraft by the seat of the pants.

During the approach, the flight control system changes to the Flare mode as the aircraft descends through 100 feet radar altitude. This change back to direct law provides more precise control inputs to counter gusty wind conditions. Control damping is still available to overcome control sensitivity.

One might think landing an aircraft the size of the A340 is a difficult task, but the opposite is true. Extremely soft landings can be made with a little experience, thanks in large part to the landing gear design. When the landing gear is extended, the rear set of wheels are hydraulically positioned lower than the front set. Upon touchdown, hydraulic pressure articulates the bogie to absorb nose-down forces. The result is three distinct touchdowns in the aircraft; the rear bogie wheels, the front ones, and the nose gear. Early A340s experi-

The uncluttered pilot positions in the A340 lead to an organized environment. The sidestick controller and steering tiller are located on the side console, with holders for aircraft manuals aft of that. The red button on the stick is an instinctive disconnect for the autopilot, and requires only a quick push to do so. If the button is pushed and held in, Sidestick Priority is activated and allows one of the pilots to take over control of the aircraft. After 30 seconds, the button need not be held down. (Scott E. Germain)

VISUAL APPROACH

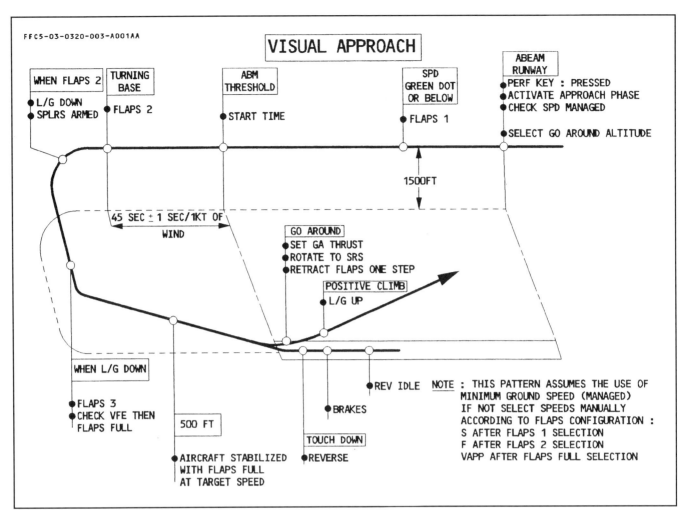

WHEN FLAPS 2
- L/G DOWN
- SPLRS ARMED

TURNING BASE
- FLAPS 2

ABM THRESHOLD
- START TIME

SPD GREEN DOT OR BELOW
- FLAPS 1

ABEAM RUNWAY
- PERF KEY : PRESSED
- ACTIVATE APPROACH PHASE
- CHECK SPD MANAGED
- SELECT GO AROUND ALTITUDE

1500FT

45 SEC ± 1 SEC/1KT OF WIND

GO AROUND
- SET GA THRUST
- ROTATE TO SRS
- RETRACT FLAPS ONE STEP

POSITIVE CLIMB
- L/G UP

WHEN L/G DOWN
- FLAPS 3
- CHECK VFE THEN FLAPS FULL

- REV IDLE

NOTE : THIS PATTERN ASSUMES THE USE OF MINIMUM GROUND SPEED (MANAGED) IF NOT SELECT SPEEDS MANUALLY ACCORDING TO FLAPS CONFIGURATION :
S AFTER FLAPS 1 SELECTION
F AFTER FLAPS 2 SELECTION
VAPP AFTER FLAPS FULL SELECTION

- BRAKES

500 FT

TOUCH DOWN

- AIRCRAFT STABILIZED WITH FLAPS FULL AT TARGET SPEED
- REVERSE

Procedure for a visual approach. (Airbus)

ILS APPROACH

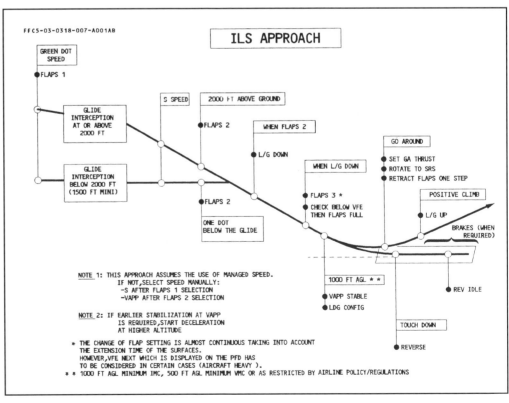

GREEN DOT SPEED
- FLAPS 1

GLIDE INTERCEPTION AT OR ABOVE 2000 FT

S SPEED

2000 FT ABOVE GROUND
- FLAPS 2

WHEN FLAPS 2
- L/G DOWN

GLIDE INTERCEPTION BELOW 2000 FT (1500 FT MINI)

- FLAPS 2

ONE DOT BELOW THE GLIDE

WHEN L/G DOWN
- FLAPS 3 *
- CHECK BELOW VFE THEN FLAPS FULL

GO AROUND
- SET GA THRUST
- ROTATE TO SRS
- RETRACT FLAPS ONE STEP

POSITIVE CLIMB
- L/G UP

BRAKES (WHEN REQUIRED)

- REV IDLE

1000 FT AGL * *
- VAPP STABLE
- LDG CONFIG

TOUCH DOWN
- REVERSE

NOTE 1: THIS APPROACH ASSUMES THE USE OF MANAGED SPEED.
IF NOT, SELECT SPEED MANUALLY:
-S AFTER FLAPS 1 SELECTION
-VAPP AFTER FLAPS 2 SELECTION

NOTE 2: IF EARLIER STABILIZATION AT VAPP IS REQUIRED, START DECELERATION AT HIGHER ALTITUDE

* THE CHANGE OF FLAP SETTING IS ALMOST CONTINUOUS TAKING INTO ACCOUNT THE EXTENSION TIME OF THE SURFACES.
HOWEVER, VFE NEXT WHICH IS DISPLAYED ON THE PFD HAS TO BE CONSIDERED IN CERTAIN CASES (AIRCRAFT HEAVY).
* * 1000 FT AGL MINIMUM IMC, 500 FT AGL MINIMUM VMC OR AS RESTRICTED BY AIRLINE POLICY/REGULATIONS

The profile flown for an Instrument Landing System (ILS) approach. (Airbus)

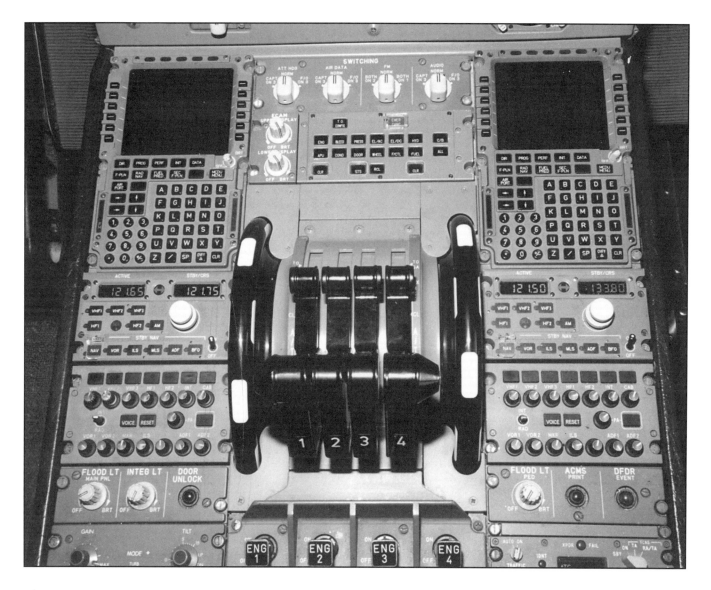

The upper center pedestal contains the ECAM control panel and switching knobs for air data, flight management, attitude data, and radio switching. The boxes below the MCDUs are Radio Control Panels, and allow each installed radio to be manually tuned. Audio Control Panels, mounted below, allow any radio to be selected and monitored. (Scott E. Germain)

enced firm nosewheel contact with the runway, but modifications to the nose gear and flight control software have solved the problem. The shorter A340-200, with a more pronounced -1.6° nose-down attitude, was susceptible to this.

The actual flare begins at approximately 40 ft. AGL to arrest the descent rate. As the auto-callout voice passes through 30 feet, the thrust levers are retarded to the idle detent, and very small stick inputs modulate pitch to allow a smooth touchdown.

After the rear wheels touch, the pilot must still fly the rest of the aircraft down to the runway. Enough elevator effectiveness remains to gently lower the nosewheel.

Once the aircraft is on the runway, small tabs on the thrust levers are brought up, allowing the thrust levers to be brought back into the reverse range. System logic prevents asymmetric application of reverse thrust on the outboard engines. With a landing weight a little more than 400,000 lbs., the effective brakes stop

the aircraft in a surprisingly short distance. Centerline control is easy with brake and rudder pedal nosewheel steering. The tillers are only used to exit the runway and for taxi turns.

Although the FBW brake system does not have any feedback, pedal force allows application without any tendency to grab or bind. The antiskid system works extremely well, and prevents any of the main wheels from reaching a skid condition. Autobrakes can be selected for landing to control braking on wet or con-

taminated runways. LO and MED positions are normally used for landing. MAX can be selected for landing emergencies, but is generally used for takeoff. LO and MED settings apply braking action at a deceleration rate of 5.9 ft/sec^2 and 9.8 ft/sec^2 respectively.

Handling an engine failure during takeoff is not an especially difficult task in the aircraft. Failure of an outboard engine at V_1 is accompanied by the appropriate warning and ECAM indications. The absent 34,000 lbs. of thrust on one side is noticeable, but easily controlled with rudder. Without any visual cues to yaw, the pilot must use the Beta target on the PFD, a symbol analogous to the turn and slip ball in other aircraft. Uncoordinated yaw is displayed by the bottom portion of the target sliding opposite the failed engine. "Stepping on the Beta Target" is a popular way of remembering which rudder to press to achieve coordinated flight. Rudder trim is used to remove the associated pedal force. If the autopilot is engaged, it will automatically trim for the engine-out condition. Once the appropriate ECAM checklist are run, the flight crew will select CONF 3 on the MCDU LDG PERF page, telling the aircraft it is landing with only three operating engines and a reduced flap setting. The FMGS will generate and display the appropriate airspeeds for landing.

If two engines on the same side fail, a surprising amount of rudder is required to maintain heading. Leveling at the initial altitude, the autothrust system will automatically set power to maintain the selected airspeed. With this change in thrust, the pilot must modulate rudder and pitch forces to maintain a stable flight condition. The initial result with new Airbus pilots is a series of pilot-induced oscillations and over controlling. If a dual engine failure occurs with an autopilot engaged, it will control the aircraft and automatically trim the rudder.

For a large, four-engine widebody, the A340 flies like a much smaller aircraft, a compliment to the flight control engineers at Airbus. Pilots must consider small inputs to the flight control stick, and resist the urge to make large corrections. Overall, pilots will spend little time getting used to flying the aircraft, as most attention will be focused on mastering the autoflight system.

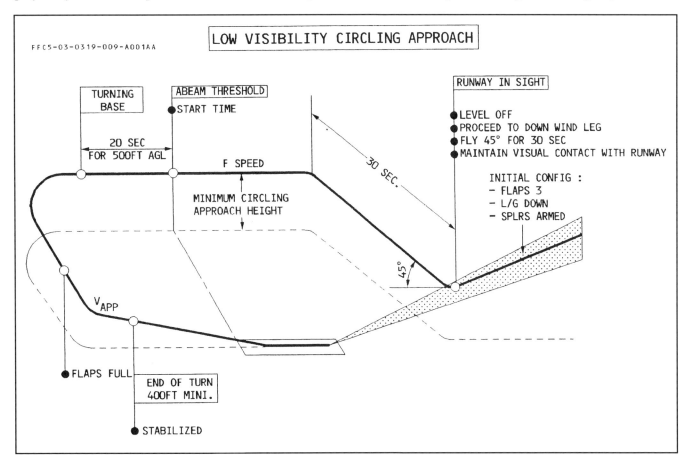

Although not performed much in the real world, the A340 is maneuverable enough to fly an instrument approach, and then circle to land on another runway. (Airbus)

It's difficult to spot the differences between the A340-200 and -300. The short-fuselage -200 contains four windows aft of door 2L, while the longer -300 sports eight. (Karl Cornil)

A Singapore Airlines CELESTAR A340-300 touches down with a small cloud of smoke. Braking and reverse thrust can be used immediately as long as the main gear bogies are compressed. (Warbird Aero Services Collection)

On takeoff, a combined 136,000 lbs. of thrust allows good acceleration to flying speed. As the nose of the aircraft rotates, the articulating main landing gear bogies provide pitch trimming and prevent tail strikes. (Mike Bednar)

Based in Colombo, Sri Lanka, AirLanka operates a small fleet of four A340-300s. As a replacement for aging L-1011s, the A340 is fulfilling one of the main roles it was designed for. Captured at Zurich, Switzerland, A340-300 4R-ADA was the first aircraft delivered to the carrier. (Mike Bednar)

An A340-300 prototype poses for the camera during the flight test program. Airbus, in marketing the aircraft to the airlines, touted it as the longest ranged airliner in the world. Its four engines actually lead to increased efficiency on long routes and ease overwater certification. The -300 carries 295 passengers in three classes, with a high-density seating capacity of 440 passengers. (Airbus)

The A340 flight control system automatically begins in Direct Law for the takeoff, allowing a direct sidestick to flight control relationship when close to the ground. The computers blend in the change to the Normal Law as the aircraft climbs and accelerates. (Mike Bednar)

Manufactured by Dowty Gloucester under a British Aerospace contract, the first main landing gear set is delivered to Toulouse. The landing gear, largest ever made for an airliner as of the early 1990s, features an articulating bogie and a shortening mechanism. (Airbus)

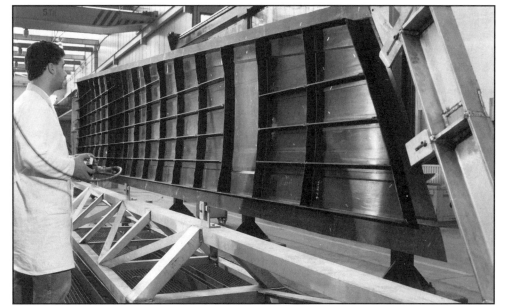

Spanish CASA is responsible for the manufacture of the A340's tail, with assembly taking place at Getafe facility. Except for the aluminum alloy center section, the entire tail is made of carbon fiber material as shown here. (Airbus)

British Aerospace workers lower a section of the A340's rear wing spar into an assembly jig at the Filton plant. The entire wing structure is completed, then flown to Germany to have flaps, slats, and equipment fitted. (Airbus)

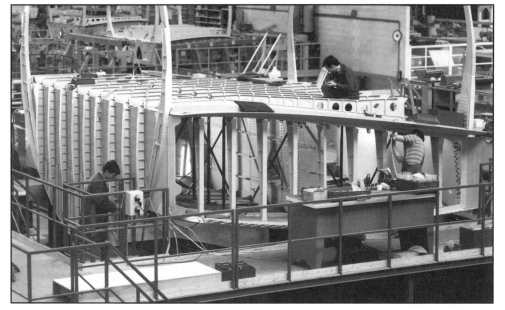

Aerospatiale's Nantes factory produces, among other things, the wing and fuselage center sections. This component is the first structure built for each A340. The deepness of the wing can be appreciated as compared to the size of the workers in the photo. (Airbus)

One wing for the first A340 is loaded on to the Super Guppy in August, 1990. The Guppies, and now the A300-600 Belugas, are key ingredients to the Airbus production process. By scheduling components to arrive for final assembly just as they are needed, costs for stocking parts and inventory are greatly reduced. (Airbus)

The "002" signifies A340 No. 2, seen taking shape at the general assembly station in the Toulouse Clément Ader facility. A340 No. 1 is visible in the background. (Airbus)

The structural shell of the first A340, built by Deutsche Airbus in Hamburg, Germany, is equipped with electrical, hydraulic, and pneumatic systems before being transported to St. Nazaire. Once there, the nose section is attached and sent to Toulouse for final assembly. (Airbus)

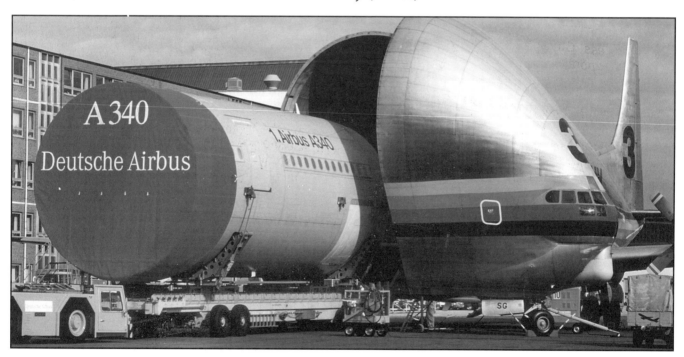

As final assembly of A340 No. 1 neared, the Super Guppies were kept busy transporting parts and assemblies between the different facilities. The volume of the specially-designed turboprops made them ideal for Airbus' modular, multi-national production process. Today, specially designed A300-600 Beluga's perform the job with more reliability. (Airbus)

Another view of A340 final assembly, where use is made of cranes and gantries which encase the aircraft once the parts are aligned. (Airbus)

Dubbed "The World Ranger," the A340 has the range to live up to the name. The aircraft completed a one stop around-the-world flight in 48 hours and 22 minutes; the fastest for any subsonic airliner. The June 18, 1993 flight also set a record for the longest flight by an airliner – Auckland to Paris – for a distance of 10,392 nm. (Airbus)

A340-300 F-WWAI poses for a shot at Toulouse during flight test. The nose-down attitude of the A340 led to flight control software changes to prevent the nose from coming down too quickly on landing. (Airbus)

A340 flight test ranged over the globe as navigation system test took place. An A340 was the first Airbus to overfly the North Pole on August 10, 1992 as part of these successful trials. (Airbus)

Flight characteristics of the A340 have been described as "easy" and "simple," due in part to the FBW computers and side stick controllers. Even in the landing configuration, the aircraft's feel remains the same as other phases of flight. (Karl Cornil)

Landing and taxi lights are bolted to the nose landing gear, and provide a wide swath of light during night operations. The headset hung on the steering actuator allows the ground tug crew to maintain communication with the flight deck crew during pushback and engine start. (Scott E. Germain)

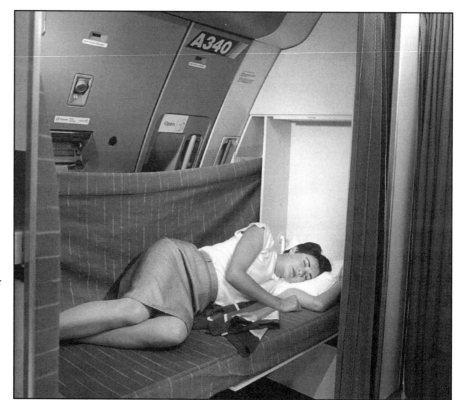

An optional fold out bunk in front of certain cabin doors provides rest areas for the cabin crew. Although curtains are installed, pesky passengers will no doubt intrude while looking for the bar, galley, or lavatory. (Airbus)

FUTURE DEVELOPMENTS

When the A340 was launched, it filled a market niche and enjoyed little direct competition. Seen as a long-range aircraft similarly sized to the DC-10 and L-1011, the A340 offered a more modern design, efficiency, and better revenue generating ability. Even though the MD-11 was launched earlier, its performance numbers were no match for the A340. Later, the launch of Boeing's 330-seat 777 generated new competition for the Airbus, and forced the company to look ahead. Demand for more payload and range from the airlines was also considered.

Future growth was always a factor when engineers designed the early -200/300 series aircraft. Since the thick wing allowed more structure to be added, higher takeoff weights could be supported by additional span on later versions. The possibility of a wing box insert, to increase wing chord and area, would also be feasible. Bolting on additional fuselage frames would be easy with the modular production process, and recent advances in engine technology would support the thrust requirements of a heavier aircraft. The A340 was perfectly positioned for growth.

After certificating the A340-200 and -300, attention turned to versions with more capacity, range, and payload. Early ideas centered on the A340-8000, a heavier 8,000 nm range version of the -200. A larger A340-400 was also moving forward, being offered to interested parties in 1996. As market demand and aircraft capabilities shifted, these two versions were superseded by the A340-500 and A340-600 variants. The program for the new airliners was launched in November 1997.

The primary goal of the A340-500 and -600 models was to offer more seat capacity and even longer

Emirates has ordered 37 Airbus aircraft, six of them being A340-500s. (Airbus)

An artist's rendering of the next-generation A340s. The -600 (below) will fly first, with the -500 (above) following quickly. Powered by Rolls Royce Trent turbofans, the new A340s will provide airlines with increased capacity; a capability that places the aircraft in direct competition with the current 747 and 777 models. (Airbus)

An artist's rendering of the A340-600 in Egypt Air livery. The airline now operates three A340s configured to carry 282 passengers in three cabin classes. Delivery of the A340-600s will occur in early 2003. (Airbus)

ranges. The new Airbuses will be the longest-ranged commercial jets in the sky, and presented the first real challenge to the current 747 market. By stretching the A340 and making other changes, the A330/340 family now challenges all 747 models in addition to the newer 777. Aggressive marketing highlighted the A340's efficiency, flexible cabin design, and fleet commonality.

As of October of 1996, Airbus froze the A340-600 design and announced a tentative service entry date in late 2002. David Pound, then the A330/340 Program Manager said, "The A340-600 is meeting the airlines' requirements while using their own methodology. At the same time, we're keeping within our limits of minimum change/maximum commonality." As Boeing has also learned, allowing the airlines to have a hand in the design of a new aircraft has great benefits.

The A340-600 is to be powered by four turbofans in the 50,000 - 60,000 lb. thrust class. Early on, different versions of the CF-6 were discussed with General Electric, but those talks failed to produce any commitments. Airbus then named the 56,000 lb. thrust Rolls-Royce Trent 556 as the chosen engine for the aircraft.

As a growth version of the A340-300, the -600 design underwent a multitude of changes. Wing chord has been increased by the addition of a wing box insert, requiring lengthening the center fuselage wing attachment points by 5 ft. 3 in. Span was increased to 208 ft. 8 in. with sweepback increasing slightly to 31.1° at quarter chord. Additional frames stretch the fuselage by 19 ft. 3 in. ahead of the wing and, 10 ft. 6 in. behind the wing for a total length of 241 ft. 1 in. Gross takeoff weight will be 804,960 lbs.

Additional aerodynamic requirements, stemming from the more powerful engines, have lead to the lengthening of the rudder by 3 ft. 3 in. and the use of the taller A330-200 vertical stabilizer. Horizontal stabilizer area was also increased to provide more tail force. A new centerline landing gear, incorporating a four-wheel bogie with brakes, is included.

Fuel capacity in the -600 will allow the aircraft to fly 7,400 nm. No changes to the flight deck or flight control laws are anticipated, and although different limiting speeds would be placarded, cross-qualification of pilots would be preserved. Air Canada, EVA Air, and Virgin Atlantic have signed on as launch customers.

A 313 seat A340-500 is also being developed, with emphasis being placed on ultra-long range operations. Launched at the 1997 Paris Air Show, the A340-500 is

Artist's concepts of the A340-500 and -600 in flight. The -500 will be the longest range airliner in the world, with a 8,500 nm. reach. The -600, farthest in the photo, will rival the size of the 747. (Airbus)

powered by four 53,000 lb. thrust Rolls-Royce Trent 553s, and features a range of 8,500 nm. Shorter fuselage plugs are used in the -500, measuring only 1 ft 9 in. ahead of the wing, and 3 feet 5 in. aft of the wing. Total fuselage length is 222 ft. 9 in. The same airframe changes made to the -600 are incorporated in the -500. Maximum takeoff weight is 804,675 lbs.

The Future

Airbus forecasts a generic market for 3,600 aircraft with 250 - 400 seats over the next 20 years. With the A330/340 family firmly placed within those boundaries, Airbus possesses an excellent aircraft to capture a good share of the market. As of this writing, Airbus has orders on the books for 537 A330/340 aircraft from 53 operators.

Although in service for a relatively short period of time, the A340 is proving to be an efficient aircraft to operate and a favorite among pilots and passengers. Its safety record has been excellent, as a major, in-service accident has not occurred. The only loss of an airline-operated aircraft to date occurred when a Sabena A340, leased to Air France, burned on the ground during maintenance. No in-flight accidents have occurred.

The Airbus story, from the early days of the A300, up through the A310, the A320 family, and the A330/A340 has been an incredible success story in terms of aircraft design and capturing market share. Politics aside, credit must be given to the manufacturer for producing solid aircraft with forward-thinking ideas. By studying the history of jetliner production, Airbus executives knew they must deliver on their promises, and listen to their customers. They have.

More and more, the general public is realizing that the "Airbus" is not simply one aircraft, but a whole family with widely differing capabilities and ranges. Pilots, mechanics, and enthusiasts often use "The Bus" in referring to any Airbus aircraft, but with such a comprehensive product line, this general term no longer applies. In 1998, half of the dollar amount of aircraft orders was taken by Airbus, and 1999 saw an improvement to 60% of the total airliner order value.

With the go-ahead on the A340-

500 and -600 models, Airbus now looks to the future and the requirement of a Very Large Aircraft (VLA). The A3XX is currently in the research and development phase, with study being conducted on powerplants, infrastructure, and market demand for the 500 - 1,000 seat aircraft. Time will tell if such an aircraft is actually feasible, but it is certain Airbus has the technology, ability, and experience to deliver.

Called the Preferred Economy Class, this section of the A340 cabin can be configured with eight-abreast seats. The overhead bins contain plenty of space for carry-on bags, as well as air vents, reading lights, and call buttons. (Airbus)

The new generation A340s will be every bit as opulent as the -200/300 aircraft. The sleeper seats shown here fold back, while foot rests extend forward. (Airbus)

Airbus planners think the future holds the requirement for a Very Large Aircraft (VLA). Research and development work is proceeding on the A3XX, a double deck aircraft capable of carrying between 500 and 800 passengers. Aerospace companies in Europe, the United States, Commonwealth of Independent States, and Asia will combine forces to produce the aircraft. (Airbus)

DaimlerChrysler tests a 1/11th scale model of the A340-500 in a low speed wind tunnel. Notice the larger Trent engine cowlings and the four-wheel center bogie. (Airbus)

APPENDICES

The following airlines operate A340s or have A340s on order (*):

Aerolineas Argentinas
Air Canada
Air China*
Air France
Air Mauritius
All Nippon*
Austrian Airlines
Cathay Pacific
China Eastern
China Southwest
Edelweiss Air*
Egyptair
Emirates
Gulf Air
Iberia
Kuwait Airways
Lufthansa
Olympic Airways
Philippine Air Lines
Qatar Airways
Qatar Amiri Flight
Sabena
Singapore Airlines
Sri Lankan (AirLanka)
Swissair*
TAP Air Portugal
Turkish Airlines
UTA*
Virgin Atlantic

	A340-200	A340-300	A340-500	A340-600
Typical Passenger Load	239	295	313	380
First/Business/Economy	16 / 42 / 181	12 / 42 / 241	12 / 42 / 259	12 / 54 / 314
Max Passenger Load	420	440	440	485
Range w/ Typical Load	8,000 nm	6,400 nm	8,500 nm	7,500 nm
LD3 Container Capacity	18 - 19	32 - 33	30 - 31	42 - 43
Launch Date	June 1987	June 1987	December 1997	December 1997
First Delivery	June 1993	February 1993	2002	Early 2002
Engines	4 CFM56-5C4	4 CFM56-5C4	4 RR Trent 553	4 RR Trent 556
Thrust	34,000 lbs. each	34,000 lbs. each	53,000 lbs. each	56,000 lbs. each
Fuselage Diameter	18.5 ft.	18.5 ft.	18.5 ft.	18.5 ft.
Length	195 ft.	208.8 ft.	222.5 ft.	246.4 ft.
Wingspan	197.8 ft.	197.8 ft.	208.2 ft.	208.2 ft.
Height	55.2 ft.	55.2 ft.	56.1 ft.	56.7 ft.
Wing Area	3,890 sq. ft.	3,890 sq. ft.	4,707 sq. ft.	4,707 sq. ft.
Wing Sweep	30°	30°	31.1°	31.1°
Optimum Cruise Speed	.82 Mach	.82 Mach	.83 Mach	.83 Mach
Maximum Speed	.86 Mach	.86 Mach	.86 Mach	.86 Mach
Maximum Takeoff Weight	606,300 lbs.	573,200 - 606,300 lbs.	804,700 lbs.	804,700 lbs.
Maximum Landing Weight	407,800 lbs.	418,900 lbs.	520,300 lbs.	560,000 lbs.
Operating Empty Weight	278,900 lbs.	286,400 - 288,100 lbs.	375,600 lbs.	390,200 lbs.
Maximum Payload	67,900 lbs.	95,900 lbs.	95,500 lbs.	123,000 lbs.
Maximum Fuel Capacity	40,960 US Gal.	37,380 - 39,300 US Gal.	56,750 US Gal.	51,500 US Gal.

Source: Airbus Industrie

Simply reading about the Airbus A340 requires the reader to be fluent in the acronyms the company uses to describe the aircraft, autoflight capability, and the display screens. Below are a list of acronyms Airbus pilots, mechanics, and designers use.

AC	Alternating Current
ACP	Audio Control Panel
ADF	Automatic Direction Finder
ADIRS	Air Data Inertial Reference System
ADIRU	Air Data Inertial Reference Unit
AGL	Above Ground Level
AOA	Angle of Attack
APU	Auxiliary Power Unit
BAT	Battery
BSCU	Brake Steering Control Unit
CBMU	Circuit Breaker Monitoring Unit
CG	Center of Gravity
CIDS	Cabin Intercommunication Data System
CLB	Climb
CONF	Configuration
CRC	Continuous Repetitive Chime
CRT	Cathode Ray Tube
CRZ	Cruise
CSTR	Constraint
DC	Direct Current
DES	Descent
DH	Decision Height
DISC	Disconnect
DISCH	Discharge
DSCS	Door Slide Control System
ECAM	Electronic Centralized Aircraft Monitoring
ECON	Economy
EFIS	Electronic Flight Instrumentation System
EIS	Electronic Instrumentation System
EMER	Emergency
EPR	Engine Pressure Ratio
ESS	Essential
E/WD	Engine / Warning Display
EXT PWR	External Power
FADEC	Full Authority Digital Engine Control
FAF	Final Approach Fix
FCU	Flight Control Unit
FD	Flight Director
FLX TO	Flex Takeoff
FMA	Flight Mode Annunciator

FMGC	Flight Management Guidance Envelope Computer
FMGS	Flight Management Guidance System
F-PLN	Flight Plan
FPA	Flight Path Angle
FPV	Flight Path Vector
HYD	Hydraulic
IDG	Integrated Drive Generator
IR	Inertial Reference
KTS	Knots – Nautical Miles Per Hour
LRU	Line Replaceable Unit
MCDU	Multipurpose Control and Display Unit
MCT	Maximum Continuous Thrust
MDA	Minimum Descent Altitude
M_{MO}	Maximum Mach number
MSL	Mean Sea Level
MTOW	Maximum Takeoff Weight
MZFW	Maximum Zero Fuel Weight
ND	Navigation Display
NDB	Non-Directional Beacon
NM	Nautical Mile
NWS	Nose Wheel Steering
OUTB	Outboard
OXY	Oxygen
PERF	Performance
PFD	Primary Flight Display
PRIM	Primary Flight Control Computers
PROG	Progress
PROT	Protection(s)
RAT	Ram Air Turbine
RMP	Radio Management Panel
SEC	Secondary Flight Control Computers
SPD	Speed
SRS	Speed Reference System
STBY	Standby
TOGA	TakeOff/Go-Around Thrust
V_1	Critical Engine Failure Speed
V_2	Takeoff Safety Speed
V_{LS}	Lowest Selectable Speed
V_{MO}	Maximum Air Speed in Knots
VOR	Very High Frequency Omni Range
V_{REF}	Landing Reference Speed
VSI	Vertical Speed Indicator
WPT	Waypoint
XFR	Transfer
ZFCG	Zero Fuel Center of Gravity
ZFW	Zero Fuel Weight

	A340-200	A340-300	B777-200	B777-300	B747-400	MD-11
Typical Passenger Load	239	295	305	368	421	298
Range w/ Typical Payload	8,000 nm	6,400 nm	4,930nm	6,510 nm	7,284 nm	4,500 nm
LD3 Storage	26	33	32	20	30	32
Engines	4 CFM56	4 CFM56	GE90 PW 4090 RR Trent 890	GE90-92 PW 4098 RR Trent 890	4 PW 4056 4 CF-6 RR RB211	3 CF-6 3 PW 4460
Thrust Rating	34,000 lbs.	34,000 lbs.	≈ 98,000 lbs.	≈ 98,000 lbs.	≈ 58,000 lbs.	≈ 62,000 lbs.
Fuselage Diameter	18.5 ft.	18.5 ft.	20.4 ft.	20.4 ft.	NA	19.9 ft.
Length	195 ft.	208.8 ft.	209.1 ft.	242.4 ft.	231.10 ft.	202.2 ft.
Wingspan	197.8 ft.	197.8 ft.	199.9 ft.	199.9 ft.	211.5 ft.	169.6 ft.
Height	55.2 ft.	55.2 ft.	60.4 ft.	60.4 ft.	63.8 ft.	57.9 ft.
Wing Area	3,890 ft.^{2}	3,890 ft.^{2}	4,628 ft.^{2}	4,628 ft.^{2}	5,825 ft.^{2}	3,648 ft.^{2}
Wing Sweep	30%	30%	31.6%	31.6%	37.3%	35%
Cruise Mach	.82 Mach	.82 Mach	.84 Mach	.84 Mach	.85 Mach	.87 Mach
MTOW	606,300 lbs.	606,300 lbs.	545,000 lbs.	660,000 lbs.	875,000 lbs.	625,000 lbs.
MLW	407,800 lbs.	418,900 lbs.	459,604 lbs.	623,535 lbs.	574,000 lbs.	430,000 lbs.
Empty Weight	278,900 lbs.	288,100 lbs.	316,800 lbs.	352,200 lbs.	399,000 lbs.	286,965 lbs.
Maximum Payload	67,900 lbs.	90,400 lbs.	63,987 lbs.	77,203 lbs.	114,300 lbs.	113,035 lbs.
Maximum Fuel Capacity	40,960 Gal.	39,300 Gal.	44,700 Gal.	45,220 Gal.	53,985 Gal.	38,615 Gal.

* *All figures for this graph are maximum values for comparison purposes. Some figures may be lower with different cabin, fuel, and equipment installations.*

With a Dornier Alpha Jet flying chase, an A340 prototype flies with slats and flaps extended during handling evaluations. The flight test program experienced few hurdles, and proceeded on track thanks to real-time telemetry and the ability to make airborne changes to flight control computers. (Airbus)

AIRBUS INDUSTRIE
AIRBUS A340

SIGNIFICANT DATES

December 1970
Airbus created.

October 1972
A300 first flight.

May 1974
Revenue airline service with A300 begins.

April 1982
A310 first flight.

March 1984
A320 program launched.

February 1987
A320 first flight.

June 1987
A330/340 program launched.

August 1988
First metal cut for A340 wing box.

December 1988
1,000 days' worth of A340 wind tunnel testing wraps up.

January 1989
Orders total 157 A330/340 aircraft. Fabrication of the first wing begins.

February 1989
Lufthansa orders additional A340s.

March 1989
TAP Air Portugal orders the A340.

April 1989
Automated riveters installed on A340 production line.

August 1990
First wing set leaves BAe for completion in Germany.

October 1990
Clément Ader Final Assembly facility is christened in Toulouse.

March 1991
First A340 leaves final assembly bay.

June 1991
Vibration tests completed, final assembly and outfitting begins.

October 4, 1991
A340 Rollout.

October 25, 1991
A340 First Flight.

January 1992
Lufthansa accepts first A340, aircraft used in flight test.

December 1992
JAA certification.

February 1993
FAA certification.

September 1993
Air France begins A340 service.

June 1997
A340-600 and -500 launched.

December 1997
Go ahead given to A340-500/600. Virgin Atlantic first airline to issue a firm order for A340-600 model.

These robotic riveters, called "automats" by Airbus employees, are used to drill 2,600 holes for bolts that connect the wings to the fuselage center section. Each automat selects one of 23 different pneumatically driven drills, attaches it to the drilling template, and disconnects. The drill is left to make the hole while the robot goes on to the next one. An additional 1,600 holes are hand-drilled by workers that can access tight spaces. All bolts are hand tightened. (Airbus)